Seize The Future For Your Business

■ SMART STRATEGIES SERIES ■

Seize The Future For Your Business

Using Imagination To Power Growth

Beth Rogers

INTERNATIONAL THOMSON BUSINESS PRESS
I⟨T⟩P® **An International Thomson Publishing Company**

London ● Bonn ● Boston ● Johannesburg ● Madrid ● Melbourne ● Mexico City ● New York ● Paris
Singapore ● Tokyo ● Toronto ● Albany, NY ● Belmont, CA ● Cincinnati, OH ● Detroit, MI

Seize The Future For Your Business

Copyright © Beth Rogers

First published by International Thomson Business Press

I(T)P® A division of International Thomson Publishing Inc.
The ITP logo is a trademark under licence

British Library Cataloguing-in-Publication Data
A catalogue record for this book is available from the British Library

Library of Congress Catalog-in-Publication Data
A catalog record for this book is available from the Library of Congress

First edition 1998

Typeset by LaserScript Limited, Mitcham, Surrey
Printed in the UK by TJ International, Padstow, Cornwall

ISBN 1–86152–203–7

International Thomson Business Press
Berkshire House
168–173 High Holborn
London WC1V 7AA
UK

International Thomson Business Press
20 Park Plaza
13th Floor
Boston MA 02116
USA

http:\\www.itbp.com

Contents

List of figures

List of tables

Introduction

Study the past, if you would divine the future.

Confucius

Hegel was right when he said that we learn from history that men never learn anything from history.

George Bernard Shaw

Business history is littered with the corpses of once great companies who missed the trends in the business environment and their own markets which were shaping the future. The past can provide, by way of analogies, an understanding of what today's companies ought to avoid and what they could aspire to. If we combine analysis of what the past and present can tell us with our own imagination and intuition, we should be able to make reasonable assumptions about how the world will develop and how our organization could succeed in it, without over-optimism or arrogance.

Microsoft is only ever two years away from failure.

Bill Gates

The premise of this book is not that company decision-makers can predict the future, but that they can deduce strong possibilities about the future and prepare for them. Considered preparation for the future can be a source of competitive advantage, and it has been one which has been sadly lacking in many organizations. In order to seize the future for our companies, we need to look beyond the normal planning parameters; certainly beyond the annual budget and even beyond the cautious 3–5 year strategic plan. We would never plan for our own futures, or our children's, on the basis of only 3–5 years. It is time to treat the organizations we work for with the same care.

Acknowledgements

Thanks to clients, colleagues, friends and family for providing anecdotal material, examples and quotes.

CHAPTER ONE

Why we need to seize the future

Personal progress through long-term planning – a recognized necessity

Because tomorrow doesn't look after itself.
Nationwide Building Society advertising slogan

Thanks to fellow human beings in the past imagining better futures, the life of man is reasonably pleasant and very long. In order to maintain our comfort, we plan for future success in our own lives – owning our own homes, comfort in retirement, career planning, and making sure the children get into the right schools and universities to ensure they get the best chances in their careers.

If you were to keep telling your family that you were not prepared to make a pension plan, that you were not going to plan for your children's education, or their health, and that you were not worried about making sure that the mortgage on the family home was paid off by the specified date, it would be no surprise if they complained about your fecklessness! Every responsible individual is expected to make long-term plans for their own retirement, and to ensure that the needs of their family will be met. We also expect to be admired for designing long-term career plans for ourselves, otherwise how could we be taken seriously by our bosses?

Almost as soon as we start work, we are encouraged to take a 40-year outlook for a pension plan. Scandals about pension mis-selling have emphasized that people need to do this thinking for themselves. When I became self-employed, I insisted that my insurance representative should calculate my plan on the basis of a retirement age of 65. At the time, the retirement age for women in the UK was 60. I assured him that I expected the law to change for women of my generation, and in due course it did. It was a simple matter of demographics and political expediency, not any psychic powers on my part. We can all make intelligent assumptions based on common knowledge such as the changing age profile of the population, and the high likelihood of politicians taking money saving options in response to it.

In the post-welfare era we are perhaps more aware than we used to be of the challenge of taking charge of our own future prosperity. We live in uncertain times. It is not enough just to get a job with the right company and keep out of trouble for 40 years. We cannot have unquestioning faith that the company will provide. In order to maximize our success in life, we seek all sorts of career advice. It is not unusual for executive careers to follow the pace of sophistication set in the sports world.

Athletes and other sportspeople today not only have to be in peak condition physically, but they also have to be mentally equipped to win. Their coaches help them to imagine themselves as winners – thinking through every aspect of the competitive event – learning how to shrug off potential problems, taking the lead, keeping the lead. Everyone who wants a prosperous life in an increasingly competitive world, in addition to constantly enhancing their applicable functional skills, has to prepare mentally in order to succeed. The purpose of this mental preparation is not just to manage potential future events – but to make the future and make sure you seize the opportunities that it offers. Preparation cannot eliminate risk and uncertainty, but it can reduce them.

One of the most commonly used techniques is to learn from past heroes. For example, Pele is an inspiration to people who love football and especially those who want to play football.

Learning from heroes of the past – Pele

Pele led the Brazilian national team to three victories in the World Cup and permanent possession of the Jules Rimet trophy. He developed outstanding kicking power and accuracy, scoring his 1,000th goal after 909 matches in top class football. Pele is a hero of world class association football, the recipient of an International Peace Award, and in 1980 he was named 'athlete of the century'.

Pele set out to promote association football in the US in 1975, and led New York Cosmos to the league championship in 1977. Many, many men around the world have lusted after football greatness. Pele truly achieved it. During his playing career, he was often asked to describe what it was that made him such a classic footballer. He would explain that whilst other footballers want to be where the ball is, 'I want to be *where the ball is going to be*'.

In our own careers, we aspire to being where the ball is going to be, and in order to secure our careers, we need to show that we can lead our companies in that direction too.

Organizational progress through long-term planning – a rare luxury

> The typical company rushes along from year to year in frenzied activity, without a clear vision of the future, and lacking distinctive or superior propositions.
>
> *Hugh Davidson, Even More Offensive Marketing*

We are happy to embrace the challenge of planning for success throughout our own long lives, but the lives of the companies we work for are still 'nasty, brutish and short'. That expression was first used by the seventeenth-century English philosopher Thomas Hobbes, who was describing human lives in those war-ravaged and disease-ridden times. In 1997, the average life of humans in Western Europe, North America and developed parts of Asia is 75–80 years. The average lifespan of a company is 40 years. Infant company mortality is as high as human infant mortality in Africa.

There are considerable changes in company league tables such as the Fortune 500 and FTSE 100 within 10 years, and the league tables of 50 years ago would be hardly recognizable. What happened to all those excellent companies of the past? Few of them made mistakes in cost management or operational efficiency. They could have hired the best accountants and project managers. It did not stop them being overtaken by rivals who had anticipated change in the way that customers' needs could be fulfilled, and produced an offer the customers could not refuse.

Of course there are organizations that have survived for a very long time. Many of these supply essential commodities, such as finance, food or fuel. In such industries, there has been an historic luxury of getting away with mistakes. That luxury has waned with the rise of consumerism. Customers are now extremely demanding. Consumers have their own lobby groups to ensure that governments impose statutory obligations on companies to provide high standards of products and service.

Technology has also had dramatic impacts on formerly comfortable industries. Banking and insurance via telephone and personal computer is imposing strains on the industry which have not yet reached their full conclusion. Hotel chains and airlines have to ask themselves whether business travellers really want to use them, or whether they would rather stay at home and video-conference with colleagues as much as is feasible. Soon, the quality and affordability of video-conferencing will enable them to do so.

No manager in any organization, even managing an 'easy' product or service, can afford one iota of complacency. Voluntary organizations and charities are also faced with the need to redefine themselves. Even the government sector, traditionally the most internally focused and often 'customer hostile' sector of economic activity, has been subject to periods of upheaval in order to improve its responsiveness and performance. So every organization has to take care to prepare for its future.

This book argues that it is possible to plan for the long-term future of an organization – openly, constructively and with reasonable expectations of getting some or most of it right. All it takes is developing a systematic understanding of what might happen by seeking and applying analogies from the past. This does not mean statistical extrapolation of past performance, but developing an understanding of what motivates change in the business environment and markets.

First of all, it is worthwhile considering some of the indicators from the past which suggest organizations might be prone to a short life expectancy.

Symptoms of short life expectancy in organizations

Only one big idea

In the nineteenth century, thousands of building societies were set up in the UK to enable their members to save to buy or build their own homes. Many wound themselves up when they had done that. Why not? They had achieved the one thing they had set out to do.

Single issue campaigns and charities have also faced this situation. A group in my county who were campaigning against motorway expansion in the area wound themselves up when they had won the argument with the government and the motorway expansion plans were shelved.

Collins and Porras (1995) have studied companies and organizations which have thrived on 'Big Hairy Audacious Goals' (BHAGs), just-believable, just-achievable visions which can provide the framework for dramatic progress. There is no doubt that BHAGs have a powerful effect, but problems may come if an organization cannot regenerate itself after the achievement of one. The company may be wound up or bought out.

Many would argue, why not? These are the dynamics of the free market and it is healthy. Some business commentators forecast shorter and shorter industry life-cycles in the twenty-first century. Indeed, it may be appropriate for some firms to set out to do one thing and then sell up.

The big idea is marvellous whilst it lasts. The greatest of them are not centred on profit, or individuals, or beating the competition – they are simple concepts, easily grasped. They are based on improving the lives of customers: reducing hassle, enhancing independence, reducing a threat, etc. They motivate people and involve people. They may have a lot in common with non-commercial quests, but they make money too. W Chan Kim and Renée Mauborgne at INSEAD have studied thirty high growth companies of the 1990s in depth and concluded that each achieved their success by providing a quantum leap in customer value.

As Hamel and Prahalad (1994) noticed, it is no coincidence that most innovation comes from start-up companies and organizations. In recent business history we think of Sun, Daewoo, Sega, Microsoft, McDonalds, Nike, Danone, Federal Express, Body Shop, PetPlan, Virgin. In the voluntary sector we think of television based appeals such as Comic Relief and Children in Need, and initiatives such as 'Fair Trade'. Davids come and fell Goliaths and then they are sometimes felled in their turn.

It is the organizations with one foot in the future, rather than those with one foot in the past, who capture the customers' imagination.

Canon seized the market for desktop copiers, not Xerox, and yet Xerox's Palo Alto laboratory is famed for great inventions. Swatch grabbed the market for pop art watches, not Seiko; and Nokia and Ericsson have the innovative reputations in the mobile phones market, rather than the giant of telecommunications, AT&T. But what happens to the innovators next?

Most established organizations would claim to aspire to continue fulfilling certain customer needs regardless of the challenge of industry change. The railway companies of the nineteenth century probably expected that they would be able to change if customers demanded it. They had been able to open up new routes, and provide different standards of service for different tastes and incomes. They had changed the world. They helped virtually every industry by getting products to market more quickly than ever before, and they accelerated the growth of new industries, such as tourism. Nevertheless, they saw themselves as railway companies, rather than fulfilling a human need to get from A to B, and were consequently eclipsed by Henry Ford and personal transport.

IBM had a presence in virtually every aspect of information systems in the 1970s. Whatever sort of system a customer wanted, IBM had the technology. It seemed implausible that 'Fortress IBM' could ever be breached. IBM had established dominance in business machines throughout the 1920s, 1930s and 1940s through inventions such as the first electric typewriter. Its second big idea, the business computer, nearly didn't happen. IBM was a follower of Remington Rand's first 'Univac' commercial computers. After the maturity of the market for mainframe computers, IBM demonstrated awareness of the markets for mini-computers, personal computers, and the software to make them accessible, but the company culture was rooted in mainframe technology. So IBM was outplayed by DEC in minis, Compaq in PCs, and Microsoft in software, and eventually lost dominance of the information systems industry to Microsoft (Figure 1.1).

This does not mean that the journalists who were writing IBM obituaries in 1991 were justified. IBM is still dominant in the provision of systems to handle masses of transactions for big businesses, and its history should enable the company to maintain success in that segment. Nevertheless, the decline of a mighty industrial empire and emergence of another caught the popular imagination around the world.

FIGURE 1.1   Product development through time – IBM

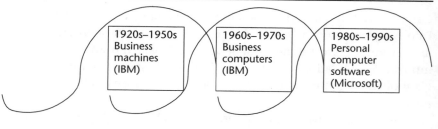

The one great leader

> Small businesses are often referred to as 'the lengthened shadow of one man.'

When small businesses grow, the power of the personality of the entrepreneur lives on. Tom Watson Senior presided over IBM's first great wave of success and Tom Watson Junior, having won the battle with his father to start building computers, presided over the second. Many people in organizations think that worrying about the future is something that only the Chief Executive should do. We want to believe that we work for a visionary leader. But, if we rely on one person, it is hardly surprising that the average lifespan of an American or European company is only forty years, about the same length as one career.

Whilst the great entrepreneur is at the helm, stakeholders feel secure. What if something happens to the person who personifies the company and the brand? The Laura Ashley retail chain has not performed well since the death of its founder in 1985. The brutal murder of Gianni Versace in 1997 prompted speculation that the company could not survive. It would be difficult for people to imagine Virgin without Richard Branson, Berkshire Hathaway without Warren Buffet, Microsoft without Bill Gates, Body Shop without Anita Roddick.

There have been, and there are some brilliant business leaders, most of whom are well aware of the pitfalls of the cult of the personality. The best guarantee for an organization to be more than 'the lengthened shadow of one man' is for everyone in an organization to learn together how to break down barriers and create new opportunities. This is the reason why business commentators have few concerns about the future of Asea Brown Boveri after Percy Barnevik, whose inspiring leadership transformed the company between 1980–97. The nature of that transformation made him a famous personality world-wide. It also resulted in a global federation of small business units with motivated employees who have strengthened ABB's global position.

Doing rather than thinking

Hamel and Prahalad (1994) found that managers spend (on average) less than 3 per cent of their time building a corporate perspective on the future. They suggest best practice would be 20–50 per cent. Most of us

FIGURE 1.2   Strategy diagram. Adapted from McDonald (1984)

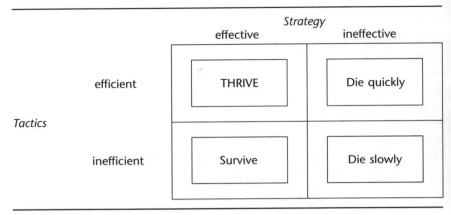

seem to feel better for doing something, rather than thinking, but without the thinking, the doing could be totally futile.

This matter of common sense is illustrated in Figure 1.2, a popular and amusing diagram for all students of strategy. If we have an ineffective strategy and pursue it with alacrity we will only hasten our organization's demise. Effective strategy is a prerequisite for survival, let alone the prospect of thriving.

Case study: 3M

3M set thinking time objectives for their employees. 3M is a company with a long history, during which it has patented some of the most innovative products in the world, has become a classic case study of the creative company and has established itself as a preferred employer. Correlation does not prove causation, but in this case the links are fairly convincing.

Cultural hostility to innovation

There are some common mistakes that companies make – in my experience it's usually to do with not reacting to change
Doug Rogers, experienced company doctor (Management Today,
August 1997)

Many company cultures are hostile to innovation because it is considered to be risky, messy and unproven. One of the most effective ways in which innovation is stifled is an obsession with seeking proof of the necessity to change through research reports and discounted cash flows. If ridiculously high rates of return are not almost certain in the short term, new projects are rejected.

If Sony had tried to test the potential for the Walkman by quantitative market research, they would probably have assumed that no market existed. Numerically presented research findings can be useful ingredients in business success, but they are not an end in itself.

Companies which are over reliant on figure-based evidence, and hostile to creativity and innovation, can only ever be market followers.

Following only the easy trends

There are armies of business academics trying to help organizations to achieve better results. They conduct research and they write books. However, it is business people who make judgements about the prescriptions offered by experts, and with true humanity, most opt for the ones which offer easy and quick relief.

In the early 1990s, organizations stampeded to implement the concept of downsizing, expecting that merely reducing the size of the organization would make it automatically more flexible and productive. There was no doubt that there was a need in those companies which had become sluggish to selectively excise unproductive functions, in which cases downsizing did deliver temporary benefits. However, flexibility and productivity also require process improvement, and many disciples of downsizing failed to make that happen.

Meanwhile, others assumed downsizing could go on for ever. One company featured on British television was asked by its holding company to find across-the-board 10 per cent savings again and again. The managers of the company finally began to reduce service to customers, and lost them as a direct result. So, the company contracted. After a management buy-out, they are now re-investing, winning customers back, and re-gaining profitability.

Professor Malcolm McDonald in 'Marketing Plans' draws the analogy between downsizing and dieting, calling the result of excess corporate dieting 'Anorexia industrialosa'. He argues that it does not take a great deal of skill to make cuts, and that managers can get hooked on the short-term success it can deliver in terms of profitability. Perhaps lack of a confident self-image leads to difficulties in understanding when to stop.

When Hamel and Prahalad said in 1994 that companies should establish intellectual leadership – which they described as making sure they have the best assumption base about the future, identifying new customer benefits and building the infrastructure to meet them – the evidence is that organizations did not rush to implement this idea. Cynics would argue that it is because intellectual leadership is much more difficult than downsizing! But, if companies do not take on difficult challenges, they cannot expect to be champions.

Lack of creative thinking skills

We find few senior management teams that can paint an enticing picture of the new industry space their company hopes to stake out over the next decade. . .

Hamel and Prahalad (1994)

There is still a reaction in most of us that future-gazing is bogus. Because we know that so many soothsayers of the past have been bogus, then the whole concept must be wrong. Soothsayers existed in the past because people had a need for a view of the future. That need has not gone away. How can an improved situation be achieved unless it is first imagined? Provided we understand and can cope with the levels of risk associated with establishing future views, and can analyse how what has been done in the past and is done today influences the future, what can be wrong with imagining the future and preparing for it?

Imagination is helped by practising creative thinking skills. There is cynicism in companies about the value of creative thinking, it is derided as 'touchy, feely', 'woolly', 'confusing', 'off-the-wall' or just plain rubbish. Many managers believe that their companies thrive on analytical and scientific thinking alone. Yet all great inventors describe their discoveries in terms of making a creative leap to imagine a possibility *before* it is tested and proven. The law of probability dictates that the more possibilities there are floating around, the more likely you are to find one which will be proven. Most ideas are after all, based on reasonable assumptions.

For example, it has been easy to imagine, since hippies and the 1973 oil crisis, that a future energy source could be solar. Solar power's share of the power market has grown painfully slowly since the 1970s, but BP stuck with their development of solar energy equipment throughout the 1970s, 1980s and 1990s. They now enjoy a substantial market share in a growing sector which is complementary to the company's traditional strengths in products which fulfil people's needs for power and warmth. John Browne, Chief Executive, commented that 'the frontier of commercial viability is always changing'.

Developing the creative thinking skills which can help to anticipate that change is a more practical approach than it at first appears.

Poor corporate mental health

Depressed people on the verge of suicide have no view of the future, or are frightened by it. Society regards depression as an illness. Most people accept that life is hard, but are nevertheless optimistic about the future, and eagerly plan for it. Dr Raj Persaud (1997) describes the three Cs of best mental health as:

- *commitment* – a sense of purpose and goals in life;

- *control* – the belief in your own ability to influence your future;

- *challenge* – accepting risk and being excited by change.

These things are often lacking in organizations. Article after article in business publications demonstrate concern about risk-averse decision-making, lack of motivation, cynicism, fear of change and fear of managers. It seems unlikely that businesses which demonstrate poor corporate mental health can survive for long in the mature, global and highly competitive markets of today.

The future is, of course, uncertain, but we must not fear it or deny it. We can learn to manage it. After all, history is also uncertain. It is constantly being adjusted by new discoveries. That does not mean to say that history should not be studied. Only by studying it more do we learn more from it, not least of all the wisdom to avoid the mistakes of history. We ought to feel the same about the future. It is not just the territory of deities, gurus or psychics. It is there for all of us to seize, for ourselves, for our organizations.

SUMMARY

With the benefit of long life expectancy, as individuals we know it makes sense to plan for our own long-term future. However, the life expectancy of the businesses we work for is, on average, comparatively short. There are many things which can lead to the death of organizations, and when the business academics get their hands on the casework, they often declare a verdict of suicide. A short lifespan may be expected if any of the following characteristics apply:

- only one big idea;

- one great leader;

- doing rather than thinking;

- cultural hostility to innovation;

- lack of creative thinking skills;

- poor corporate mental health.

We can learn from the problems experienced by other companies. This helps us to avoid known risks when we build a framework for a prosperous future for our business.

Chapter 2 discusses how famous company role models have built successful futures on successful pasts and introduces the methodology for long-term future planning.

How the future has been seized

So easy it seemed once found, which yet unfound most would have thought impossible.

John Milton

Imagining the future and then implementing it

Just as people can take measures to improve their chances of a longer life, so can companies and organizations. An external and long-term focus is required. Systematically, the health of the company can be improved by practising a practical route to the exploitation of imagination.

The good news is that long-term thinking also helps in the short term. Being consistently first to act on underlying trends can provide competitive advantage in the short term as well as the long term, and it does not preclude consideration of future cost management, efficiency and effectiveness. Also, decision-makers who have explored all aspects of possible futures can deduce the logical conclusions of all options open to them in urgent situations, and can avoid 'knee-jerk' reactions. Of course, it is easier to make good short-term decisions if the long-term direction of the organization is clear.

Expert opinion is quite explicit:

it is imagination, far more than capital, that powers growth.
Professor Gary Hamel of London Business School, quoted in the
Financial Times

Wise are they who start . . . the Pathway through Paradox, the way to build a new future while maintaining the present.

Professor Charles Handy

Business genius lies in imagining revenues that do not yet exist.

Peter Martin

Unless a company is progressing the whole time, it is, in fact, moving backwards. It is quite impossible to maintain the status quo. . .

Sir John Harvey Jones

So why don't we plan for the very long term of our organizations? Why do most business managers in the USA and Europe think themselves very far-sighted if they have a 3–5 year strategic plan rather than an annual budget? Many rival companies from the Far East have 30-year plans, some are rumoured to have 200-year plans!

The first ingredient of success is courageous ambition. Nobody I have met in successful start-up companies ever planned to do just a few percentage points more year after year. However, note that growth is not the only criterion which drives success.

It takes a great deal of determination, enthusiasm and belief to take some of the risks that will be described in the following examples. Not every company wants to operate that way. Of course, with great risks, there is a chance of failure. Sometimes, doing nothing runs a high risk of failure too, and it is never noticed until it is too late. The business that wants to seize the future takes a positive view of risk.

Example 1: Sony

In the 1950s, Sony set out to change the image of Japanese products around the world, signified by a name change which their investors at the time did not think at all necessary. By the late 1970s, Japanese products had indeed acquired a reputation for quality, an amazing contrast to the 1950s perceptions of shoddiness.

In the 1980s and 1990s, Western companies have been keen to learn about Japanese working methods. However, Sony had another ingredient besides quality processes. Akio Morita, co-founder of Sony, explains that 'Our plan is to lead the public with new products rather than ask them what kind of products they want.' Is this marketing heresy? Is it being product led rather than customer led? Not necessarily.

Sony have discovered the art of identifying unexpressed needs and developing products to fulfil them, a topic which is explored in more detail later.

Example 2: Boeing

One of the classic case studies of very long-term thinking in a Western company is Boeing, who, by courageous thinking, achieved long-term dominance of the aircraft industry by taking huge risks to fulfil expectations of future markets (Figure 2.1).

Boeing was founded in 1916, in the very early days of aeronautics, after William Boeing and his partner developed a seaplane. Through the next few decades, Boeing developed many military aircraft, including the famous B17 Flying Fortress (1935), a very literal analogy with building castles in the air! After the war, the demand for military aircraft declined. Boeing dared to make plans for a commercial jet, although there was no apparent interest from the market, especially since the Comet jet airliner, pioneered by de Havilland in 1949, was grounded in 1953 after a crash caused by metal fatigue.

The Boeing 707 first flew in 1958. During the 1960s, the 707 together with its equally risky successors, the 727 and 737 took a huge share of the world market for Boeing. Not content to rest on their laurels, Boeing followed in 1970 with the 747 Jumbo jet. The development of the Jumbo nearly bankrupted the company, but having the courage partially to cannibalize their existing 'cash cow' paid off within 10 years. Progress did not stop there. Boeing now encompasses a wide range of transport vehicles, including space vehicles, and engineering and construction services. These developments have required huge investment and involved huge risks. And Boeing is moving on again, with a vision of a

FIGURE 2.1   Product development – Boeing

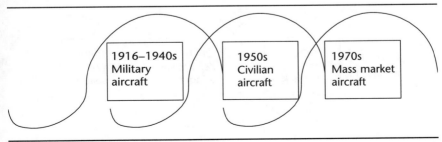

future airliner which will be more like a cruise ship than a bus, enabling the passengers to move around from lounge to lounge.

Example 3: JCB

JCB, a global supplier of agricultural and construction vehicles, has survived in a cut-throat business for over 50 years and has won fifty awards for engineering, design, marketing, management and care for the environment. The company has a 40 per cent share in Europe and a significant presence in other world markets. JCB is owned by the Bamford family, but has a strong culture to encourage everybody's ideas.

In 1946, JCB branched out from its British base and demonstrated foresight by choosing France as its first export market rather than a British colony. When the company entered the US market, no profit was returned for 13 years, but the managers were prepared to persist. They knew that the USA was the toughest single market in the world and European companies who wanted to be there had to be there for the long term.

In addition to JCB's market extension wisdom, their product innovation is legendary. They invest heavily in research and development, and encourage ideas from all employees and customers. Figure 2.2 shows their record over five decades. The Fasttrack tractor is their current

FIGURE 2.2 Product development – JCB

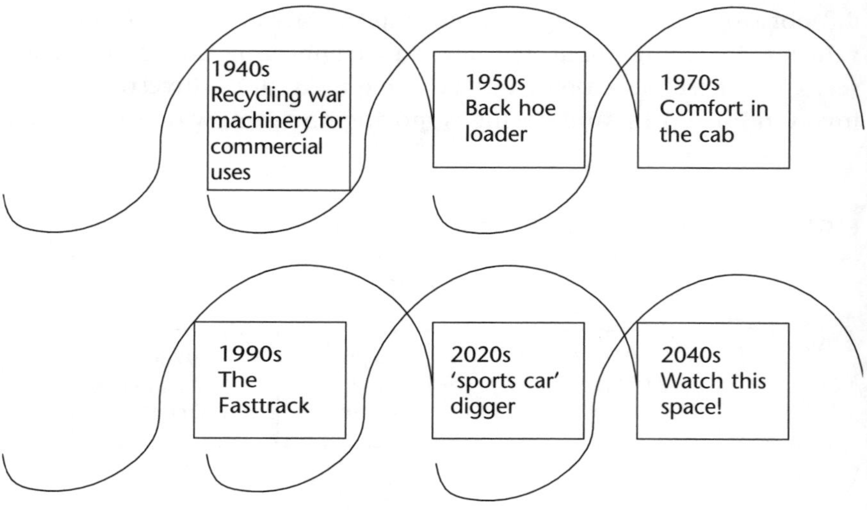

| 1940s Recycling war machinery for commercial uses | 1950s Back hoe loader | 1970s Comfort in the cab |
| 1990s The Fasttrack | 2020s 'sports car' digger | 2040s Watch this space! |

claim to fame and, as the name suggests, it goes much faster than conventional tractors – motorists need not fear getting stuck behind it on country roads! They already have a design for the next generation of diggers and tractors, with all-round visibility, high level comfort features and advanced communications with the office.

Last, but not least, JCB have employed imagination in other aspects of the business. 'The Dancing Diggers' (yes – diggers can be driven to emulate formation dancing routines!) are a remarkable public relations channel, and their environmental awards demonstrate an appreciation of social trends.

Readers may be thinking that future-gazing is, of course, entirely necessary for companies producing capital goods which cost their customers huge amounts of money, and it may be prudent if you are in a technology-driven industry such as information systems, home entertainment or medical supplies. A culture of 'seizing the future' can also help if you are providing consumer 'essentials'.

Example 4: Tesco

The grocery store Tesco was established in the east end of London in 1932 and had expanded to most London suburbs by the end of the Second World War. In 1947, the company was floated on the London Stock Exchange to finance conversion of the stores to self-service, an idea imported from the USA.

In the 1950s and 1960s, Tesco expanded throughout the UK, although food retailing was still dominated by local co-operative societies, whose members were very loyal shoppers because of the dividend they received on purchases. In the 1970s, Tesco launched an assault on its competitors through price cutting – the motto 'pile it high, sell it cheap' was born. It led to a 40 per cent increase in sales in one year.

In the 1980s, Tesco invested heavily in larger stores and new technology, from 1985–90 the capital programme totalled £1.3 billion. The company was also moving upmarket, attracting middle class shoppers with a wider, higher quality and more cosmopolitan choice of products, but managed to retain customers with constrained budgets through 'value lines'. This has resulted in a dominant market share. 1990s initiatives include re-visiting investment in smaller shops, a loyalty card and financial services, which were, ironically, all part of the history of the co-operatives.

Plans for the future seem to be centred on geographical expansion in Europe and the Far East. It also seems certain that, after early successes with limited lines, Tesco will be a pioneer of electronic shopping (Figure 2.3).

FIGURE 2.3 Product development – Tesco

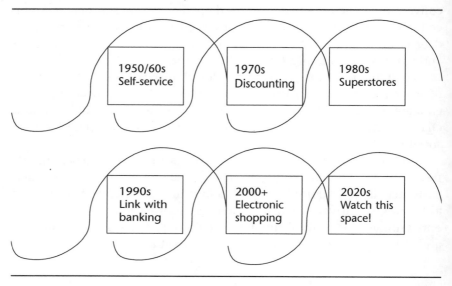

1950/60s Self-service	1970s Discounting	1980s Superstores
1990s Link with banking	2000+ Electronic shopping	2020s Watch this space!

We could all aspire to be so inspired

Carry your own lantern and you need not fear the dark.
Leo Rosten's Treasury of Jewish Quotations

The companies who continue to be admired over long periods of time are, in one way or another, systematically thinking about the far future. They are also consciously building on their own history of innovation or the history of their industry, and taking into account changing business environments and markets. They also seem to learn from mistakes and successes, their own and those of other companies. It seems that the more they do it, the better they are at it. It is not that they have never considered wrong moves: Sony, Boeing, JCB and Tesco have considered many other things besides those they have chosen to do.

The openness to many options for the future makes it easier to choose the most probable winning options, despite the risks involved.

Inspiration to generate these many options can be contrived and recreated by adopting a creative thinking process and practising it. This book describes a manageable structure for long-term planning in organizations. It is like a board game. We start our progress from the bottom left-hand corner, as shown in Figure 2.4.

It will come as no surprise to experienced planners that preparation and practice are required as a first move, just like they would be in a board game. Unlike most board games, however, long-term planning is a team effort. Everybody on the team will need to share their understanding of the company's 'now' position. Some information gathering from external sources may also be required. Then, the history of the industry and the

FIGURE 2.4 Long-term planning

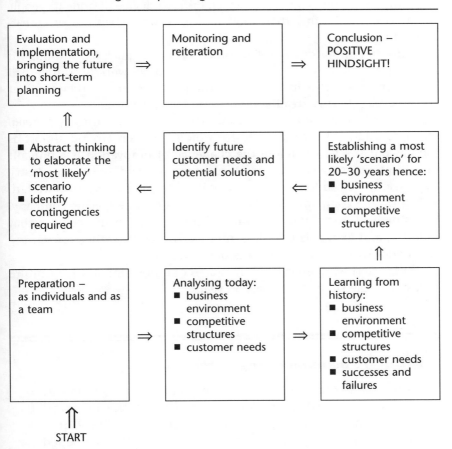

company need to be explored. The team is then in a position to compare the 'now' situation with what might have been dreamed of 20–30 years ago. That makes it easier to imagine how much change might be achieved in the next 20–30 years.

The team need to identify the drivers for change in the business environment and the competitive structures of the industry. Then, they have to devote special concentration to how the needs of customers might drive change or could be inspired to drive change by a supplier's imaginative fulfilment of their currently unexpressed needs. Further creative exploration can be ensured, both to enhance the emerging scenario and identify potential alternatives, by using abstract thinking techniques. Thereafter, the team must apply themselves to analysing and evaluating the elements of the plan which have most potential for early implementation. Over time, progress will have to be routinely monitored. The expected result is hindsight which brings a degree of pride to people in the company, rather than indifference, incomprehension or embarrassment.

Inspiration needs time. This process is not a quick fix. Although it can be introduced to a planning team in a single workshop, they will need to practise it to gain confidence using it. Over time, as they see their plans develop to drive reality, motivation levels will rise.

In explaining how the process works, I will be using a *fictional* example. I have chosen an industry which has been around almost as long as our species, therefore the challenge of innovation is a difficult one. Its products are very familiar to all of us, so regardless of our industry specialisms, we can join in with the project team of XYZ Furniture Ltd. This furniture company example is not based on any specific company, but is derived from interviews with a retired senior manager from that industry, and extrapolated using intuitive consensus gathered from my experience with other consumer goods industries.

Let's start with a review of the waves of innovation in the furniture industry in the UK over the past 50 years.

Furniture manufacturing in the UK

During the Second World War, British people had only been able to buy what was called 'utility' furniture, which was very functional. It was also rationed. 'Utility' furniture continued into the 1950s. By the late 1950s, all rationing had been abolished. It was a period of which the Prime Minister of the day was alleged to have said that 'you've never had it so good'. A few enterprising furniture manufacturers launched an assault to sweep up all the suppressed demand for home comforts. They offered affordable, stylish furniture which had never before been accessible to 'mass' markets. In terms of market leadership, the G-Plan brand was perhaps best known for encapsulating the 'spirit of the times' (in that it generated the most jokes!)

In the 1960s there was a vast, largely manufacturing-led, expansion of the market. Success was constrained by a number of factors. Successive governments tried to curtail consumer demand through purchase taxes and credit controls. The industry required highly skilled labour, and the trade unions were very strong. Whilst they did not strike, they did manage to influence production for their members' benefit. The industry was mostly in the hands of influential families who had established the industry in the nineteenth century. Whilst the furniture entrepreneurs were very bright men who knew their businesses inside out, they were disinclined to seek outside investment for expansion.

Despite these constraints, the overall factors were in the manufacturers' favour. The middle classes were growing in number and, through higher disposable income were able to change their furniture more often, following a trend which was established in the US and other parts of Europe.

During the 1950s, new technology which had been pioneered in the production of wooden aircraft during the war, was applied to furniture production, enabling particle board with a wood veneer to replace solid wood in certain items of furniture. The 1960s saw further advances in the mechanization of production, timber drying and timber preparation.

The manufacturers had two challenges in terms of segmenting their markets. One was the retail outlets for furniture. The big department stores had power in the market, and demanded special attention. It was also essential to make sure that small stores in provincial towns could offer your brand. Reasonably sophisticated market research was also applied to consumers, who were segmented by social class, and lifestyle attributes such as newspaper readership.

Having done remarkably well in the 1960s, highly branded furniture manufacturers lost their hegemony in the 1970s. A department store called 'Habitat' burst forth from its niche beginnings on 'swinging' London's most trend-setting shopping street to sweep up the custom of the nation's baby boomers setting up home for the first time. Habitat offered cheap, high fashion furniture in plastic, steel, glass and stripped pine, as well as novelties such as bean bags and floor cushions.

At the same time, do-it-yourself furniture consisting of plastic veneered chipboard panels became available through warehouse-style retail outlets. This offering was aimed at people on low incomes. Both Habitat and the DIY stores picked up on consumer demand for cheaper furniture which did not have to be ordered months in advance.

In the 1960s, the consumer who wanted to buy a cupboard could do so at a department store, or if they lived in a city, there might also be a specialist furniture shop or two. If they lived in a rural area, it was possible to buy furniture via mail order catalogues. In the 1970s, the consumer could go to a department store, a specialist shop, a warehouse outlet, a fashion store such as Habitat, a DIY furniture showroom, or use mail order.

In the 1980s and 1990s, the winners in the industry have been 'category killers', the large out-of-town furniture stores offering choice and low prices. Manufacturers' brands have very little impact in the market.

There were two means of survival for traditional furniture manufacturers throughout these changes. Offering affordable

FIGURE 2.5   Product development – XYZ Furniture

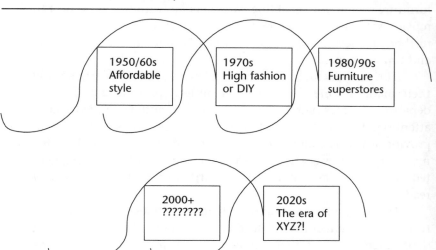

classical choices to the more mature, conservative consumer, or high price niches. In our example, XYZ Ltd has survived by the first route. Selling to the parents of the G-Plan and Habitat generations was a reasonably comfortable market position, but the discount retailers of the 1980s and 1990s have demanded very high standards for cheaper prices. Many furniture companies have gone out of business. XYZ Ltd needs a new lease of life.

First of all, the company has to put a team together who can work on its long-range planning project, which has been named XYZ+20.

SUMMARY

In this chapter we have:

■   considered a number of examples of companies who have repeatedly seized their own future;

■   introduced the board-game style approach to the long-range planning challenge;

■   introduced an industry example which will explore this process.

Chapter 3 discusses choosing and developing a project team to create future views for the company.

Choosing and developing the project team

Why individual intuition is not enough

Predicting the future is usually considered the realm of shamans, astrologers or mystics of some sort. However, from the Oracle at Delphi to modern day soothsayers, the problem is that all that is served up by these prophets, who are trying to please their audience, is very vague and does not actually seem relevant or to make you any the wiser about what you might do to seize a better future for yourself.

At Delphi, the Pythia (priestess), high on laurel leaves and the alleged properties of the natural vapours of the area, sitting on Apollo's sacred tripod, uttered incoherent cries. Intermediaries in the temple interpreted them for those who came seeking advice, but they still left the applicant guessing. King Croesus of Lydia, who had defeated the Ionian Greeks, sought advice about taking on the might of Persia. He was told that if he waged war on the Persians, he would destroy a great power. Of course, it is easy for us to sit here and say that he could have worked out for himself that in any war there is going to be a loser. He assumed the Oracle was telling him that the loser would be Persia. In fact, the great power that he destroyed was his own – his army was crushed by the Persians.

Just as Croesus alone was not able to see all the possible outcomes, it is unlikely that there is any one individual in the company able to interpret all the signs relating to its future. Even if the Chief Executive is very clever and charismatic, relying only on his or her interpretation is not enough. Thorough investigation is needed to uncover as many signs as possible, and diverse outlooks are required to ensure a variety of interpretations are explored.

Why a team?

Effective innovation was a fluid, collective process that was more likely to come from good teamwork than from a stereotypical boffin working alone in the laboratory.
From an article describing a successful change programme at Pilkington Optronics, by Bell, Blackler and Crump

It is the most natural thing for human beings to come together in groups. We are social animals. It has become almost a cliché to insist teamwork makes for the best strategy search. Psychologist Ian Morley's research indicates that creative work is a social, not a solitary activity. Also, of course, it is perceived that multi-disciplinary teams ensure widespread 'buy-in' to the outcome of the project. Yet Peter Senge, in his work on learning organizations, identified the phenomena of business teams made up of individuals with IQs over 120 demonstrating a collective IQ of 63.

What a team is not

It is important to distinguish between team working and committee working.

A camel is a horse designed by committee.

Proverb

Committee members often see themselves as delegates from interested parties mandated to behave in a certain way, or to make a biased argument, or to wheel and deal to score points. This is particularly evident in political hierarchies, especially those of political parties. Part of Tony Blair's crusade for the British Labour Party has been to lessen the role of committees and conferences and bring policy-making into workshop-style events where discussion and exploration has a chance to prevail over confrontation.

There is the danger in committees of seeing the matter in hand only in black or white. Peter Martin (1997) commented that all markets have a herd mentality, and some herds are more unthinking and destructive than others. The press apparently gave the senior partners of the top global accountancy firms involved in copycat mergers in late 1997 a very hard time. Was it strategy or was it panic at being left behind?

Committees can be places where people come together to bury initiatives in opprobrium. Committee-run companies are more interested in self-congratulation than embracing change for the future. In committees there is a culture of win–lose – 'you are either with us or against us' – a culture of public blame, and inflexibility combined cleverly with prevarication. Judgement is to be applied and plenty of it, and being there is what matters, not what you contribute.

Vested interests lead to conflict which leads to anarchic and destructive displays. Although the introduction of radio and television into parliaments around the world is claimed to have resulted in marginally improved behaviour, voters are still disdainful of what they see as 'yah-boo' methods of running their countries. The truth is that 'yah-boo' has been observed in many private organizations where politics with a small 'p' is rife.

Committee-run organizations have a tendency to waste time and then make decisions rashly. They are allowed to get away with generalities most of the time, and are then heavily criticized by customers or shareholders when they show any sign of weakness. This prompts them into action – any action, right or wrong.

Characteristics of a creative team

In creative teams, members come as themselves, and think as themselves. They do not have to prove anything to a constituency. Everybody recognizes shades of grey, and has the courage to work with them. Indeed, they recognize that confusion and uncertainty are essential to discovery. They can develop win–win solutions, encourage creative conflict, and be flexible and imaginative. The creative team has a risk-taking approach.

We made it by using the machines incorrectly.
Tony Berryman, Chairman of textiles company Welbeck, describing their
innovative, shantung fabric

The culture of the team is about problem-solving, to the extent that the team will even look for problems to solve through the constructive management of self-criticism.

Andy Grove, Intel's chief executive, has commented that continuous self-criticism, even when the markets are happy with you, is the best protection against waking up and discovering that the herd has stampeded over you.

The members of a creative team can suspend judgement when necessary for the exploration of ideas. They know that every idea deserves some space as even a superficially impossible idea may be a stepping stone to a brilliant solution.

A client told me about how he had learned the value of suspending judgement. He was involved in a team working for a Canadian utilities company. They got together to discuss the problem of heavy snow breaking overhead cables. Someone suggested that bears might be able to help, as when they rubbed themselves against the telegraph poles, it shook snow off the lines. Someone who asked themselves how the bears could be persuaded to rub themselves up against the poles suppressed their objection and suggested that honey could be put at the top of the poles to attract the bears' attention. Another person, who wondered how the honey could be got to the top of the poles, suggested that helicopters would be needed to deliver the honey. Then everyone realized that the air movement created by the helicopter would blow the snow off the lines! The solution adopted was to fly helicopters up and down the lines to remove the snow and thus save repair costs. The poor old bears missed out, but the company gained a great deal.

The creative team also operates in a culture of experimentation and tolerance of failure.

The New Zealand national rugby team has a tremendous record of winning form which stretches back 25 years into rugby history. One follower of Welsh rugby, after Wales had been soundly beaten by New Zealand, described them as 'bulldozers and ballet dancers combined.' Researchers found it paradoxical that such a winning machine could emerge from a team culture which tolerated failure. However, it is New Zealand's insistence on always taking something new to opponents that ensures that, even if not every experimental move is a success, the other team are always on the defensive.

Creative teams in business behave as if they are in a disciplined sports team, a group of specialists whose performance depends on individual flair and how they play together. They know that their collective outcome matters, so they all contribute, and take collective credit.

TABLE 3.1 The differences between a creative team and a committee

Creative team	Committee
Members come as themselves	Members come as delegates or representatives of particular interests, they come with the baggage of others
Members can cope with ambiguity, abstraction and shades of grey	Everything has to be black or white, right or wrong
Interested in win–win solutions	'If you're not with us, you're against us' – win–lose attitudes
Encourage creative conflict	Suppress conflict or exclude dissenters
Culture of experimentation, tolerance of failure	Culture of blame
Constructive self-criticism – seeking out problems to solve	Follow the herd or defer to custom and practice
Risk-taking, imaginative	Avoid innovation or risk
Flexible	Inflexible
Suspend judgement	Apply judgement and plenty of it
Output matters – so contribute	Being there is what matters, not contribution
Collective credit	Deference to the boss

The whole team

The question is not team or no team, but how to structure the team to achieve a creative atmosphere. The first dimension is to consider how wide the team of people who want the organization to succeed actually is. All the stakeholders, including shareholders, employees, customers, suppliers and the local communities in which the company operates are interested in its long-term success. Many companies and public service organizations try to involve all stakeholders in strategy search.

One of my regular clients is a small company providing technical services which is becoming increasingly commoditized by the ever-increasing pace of technology. The entrepreneur concerned saw the need to break out from this cycle if the company was going to have a prosperous future. He invited suppliers, customers and even a (geographically complementary) competitor to join him and a few key employees in the search for a 20 year outlook.

The Open University in the UK, wanted to involve as many of the 3,800 staff in forming the university's strategic plan – including academics, administrators, packers, gardeners and editors, through a programme of workshops, followed by a one-day conference. A planning team of volunteers was formed to ensure implementation. Students were also consulted.

An American utilities company invited all their employees to take part in dialogue about long-term strategy. The democratization of strategy facilitated 'breaking the rules'. It also increased the legitimacy of the values of the firm and the management of it.

Years of downsizing have had the side effect of widespread cynicism about management and managers from the very people who produce the organization's wealth. Only if all the workforce are consulted and involved will trust and respect be restored. After all, the alternative might be to go back to the 1970s which was regarded as the decade when union power and intransigence destroyed British industry. However, failure to involve shopfloor workers in strategy was part of the problem at that time.

Management/employee relationships in the 1970s

Example 1

An elected trade union representative working in the automotive industry reacted angrily when faced with a presentation from the management of the company about the need for redundancies. He insisted that if only they would give him access to the same information they had, he could show them a way to turn the company around. He did not want to destroy the company, he wanted to save jobs. Since the management believed that conflict between themselves and the union was endemic, there was no prospect of co-operation on a rescue package.

Example 2

In the UK defence industry, a group of workers got together to produce a plan for their company which would smooth the transition to non-defence production. It was ignored by their own management, but they managed to sell some of their product ideas to companies in Germany and Japan.

Research indicates that downsizing has resulted in worse employee relations than the excesses of 1970's conflict between unions and management. The workplace of the 1990s has been characterized by nastiness founded in job insecurity, lack of trust, belief in hidden agendas, cynicism and fear of asset-stripping. Teamwork is often regarded as a sham, because the company does not keep its promises, to customers or to employees. Managers at the very top have to work all the way through the organization if they want to rebuild trust. They will need persistence because it takes time. It is not possible just to make pleasant noises and expect the message to be absorbed.

It takes time, money, and a lot of hard work to convince stakeholders to trust the management of a company which has caused them pain in the past. However, it can be done, if the will exists. The advantages in terms of goodwill and positive contributions to improving company performance usually prove to be worth the effort.

The focus team

Bill Russell, a player with the Boston Celtics, said of the team during a run of 11 championships out of 13: 'Off the court, most of us were oddballs by society's standards – not the kind of people who blend in with others or who tailor their personalities to match what others expect of them.'

Besides welcoming as many contributions as possible as often as possible, a focus team is required to bring contributions together and work out the whole picture. How do we spin down from welcoming ideas from all stakeholders to the precious few who have to develop future outlooks in detail?

Part of the formula is to include people who appear to have a creative approach. Researchers who have studied people with imagination who have driven great leaps of progress, tell us that they are bored by logic but inspired by vision, more driven by emotion than analysis.

Psychologists have tried to determine whether creativity is inherited or moulded by life experiences. The parents of creative children often complain that they are physically and mentally over-active, annoyingly curious and solitary. Those characteristics probably lead to conflict in early childhood, which Lange-Eichbaum identified as a stimulus. These children would be likely to grow up into the 'industrial revolutionaries' which Hamel (1997) believes are much needed in business.

Curiosity has been acclaimed by many researchers in the field of creativity as the characteristic trait which is singularly important to idea generation. The creative individual is also independently minded, likes humour, and applies it to the challenge in hand, thus relieving tension. The creative individual can defer judgement, take risks, use imagery, tolerate ambiguity and think impulsively. This person will be committed to the truth and willing to root out the ways in which we limit or deceive ourselves. He or she will also be able to integrate reason with intuition.

Although we have an image of the highly creative person as neurotic, many of the aspects of the creative adult can be linked to aspects of emotional intelligence. Emotional intelligence is about being aware of one's own feelings, awareness of and empathy with the feelings of others. It is also about being able to manage moods, stay motivated, stay optimistic, and interact well with others. Emotionally intelligent people have listening skills and criticize constructively. They can deal with a degree of uncertainty or confusion. They are solution-oriented. In the work context, the emotionally intelligent person will be aware of fears and concerns generated by the outcome of their work and communicate to others with openness and trust.

Some organizations can take their pick of creative, emotionally intelligent people. Others, which have been constrained by bureaucratic cultures in which neither characteristic on its own or combined was particularly career-enhancing, will need to think hard about how to develop and reassure employees. Their creativity is there, but suppressed. In order to release it, a creative atmosphere can be introduced in the team. The easiest and most commonly used technique is to ensure a diversity of outlook among team members.

Building diversity into the team

> It is no mean feat to build a team that is international in perspective, and then to manage, train and develop a group of people with different backgrounds, experiences and expectations, and weld them into a cohesive team.
>
> *Lynda Brennan, senior consultant with ECA International*

Even though diversity is difficult, the alternative is even worse. Sameness in teams has to be avoided. It can lead to a dangerous phenomenon known as 'Groupthink' (Janis, 1971). 'Groupthink' is at work when any individual who expresses unusual views or presents alternatives to accepted 'norms' is ridiculed and excluded. As a result, the team ends up pursuing prejudiced solutions.

FIGURE 3.1   A diversity model – the Rubik's Cube of team choices

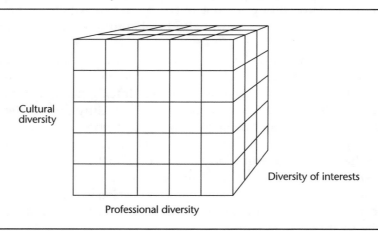

Cultural diversity

Diversity of interests

Professional diversity

Professional diversity includes:

- finance/accounting;
- sales/marketing;
- secretarial;
- engineering;
- shop floor worker.

Examples of cultural diversity are:

- country-based (e.g. German, American, Indian, Australian);
- based on economic circumstances;
- based on other issues, such as gender, disability, etc.;
- attitude-based (e.g. approach to family values, community spirit, etc.).

In the category of diversity of interests are such characteristics as:

- artistic;
- sporty;
- model-building;
- collecting;
- do-it-yourself;
- voluntary service in the community.

Each small cube within the large cube is an individual team member. As with the Rubik cube, *the individual cubes can twist and turn,* but the whole 'team' of cubes is always intact.

It is important to build capacity for learning into teams, and what could be easier than learning from other team members? Diversity is vital, even if it involves some conflict. Great teams are not characterized by lack of conflict, but in great teams, conflict becomes productive.

> The most important characteristic of firms on the rise is a bit of healthy dissent.
>
> *Professor Stopford, London Business School*

Professional diversity

Consider that:

- a sculptor invented the ball-point pen
- a veterinary surgeon invented the pneumatic tyre
- a musician invented kodachrome films
- an organist invented the seed drill

We can all think outside our narrow professional disciplines given the right environment.

The first essential aspect of diversity is to build the team from different functions in the organization. The concept of multi-disciplinary teams as a productive formula has been in circulation since the early 1960s, and there have been innumerable case studies since to support those early findings.

Diversity across line responsibility is also recommended. Most of my clients involve people from the shopfloor, secretaries, customer service clerks, etc. with great success. Involvement leads to commitment as well as diversity of ideas.

Everybody has the capacity to be creative at work.
Professor Michael West, Centre for Organizational Innovation, Sheffield University

Cultural diversity

For 90 years Chelsea Football Club enjoyed a reputation in the English League for flair without discipline or consistency, and won hardly any honours. In the mid-1990s, the team became multi-national. Two noticeable themes were Italian players to enhance the flair and a Dutch manager who ensured a disciplined framework. The team's win-rate improved dramatically.

An Australian textile company decided to take on a Bosnian refugee as a production manager. They felt that the creativity he must have learnt in an industry without parts or materials for 10 years was bound to be of value to them.

People's perceptions of the world are affected by the culture in which they have matured, that is those given factors such as nationality, religion, social attitudes and economic circumstances. When determining the future of the business, it is worthwhile employing and exploring different cultural outlooks. It is said that the greatest failing of military strategy is that it is 'ethnocentric'. An ethnocentric business strategy would be high risk in global markets. For small companies who perhaps cannot incorporate national diversity, involving stakeholders other than employees in the focus team would be a suitable alternative.

Shell, regarded as pioneers of scenario planning, perceived the need for diversity at the very birth of the process. The two core movers of scenario planning have been described as 'a Franco-German philosopher' and 'a flamboyant Argentinean gambler'. The first planning team consisted of ten different disciplines from accountancy to nuclear physics, and ten different nationalities.

Diversity of interests

Cultural perceptions are 'given', but we make choices in life too. We choose the non-work interests we pursue and the role we play in our family and among our friends. Bringing things learnt from hobbies and domestic circumstances and applying them at work can bear glorious fruit.

An IBM technician faced with the problem of packing sensitive disks as safely as possibly, applied a principle from scuba diving to the packaging and thus saved the company money and the customers from the problem of disks arriving damaged.

Akio Morita says that the inspiration for the Sony Walkman was observing his daughter's passion to have music wherever she went.

The importance of diversity of interests is such that some companies send team members on seminars relating to unusual interests as part of their preparation for creative work. However, it is important first of all to tap the interests team members already have.

Team roles

There is another ingredient, which is a very obvious factor in all sports teams, but is not always applied in business teams.

Higher productivity can be achieved where each of the members can assume a complementary behavioural role in the team. Dr R Meredith Belbin spent many years examining patterns of behaviour in management teams, and identified roles which people prefer depending on their character. The roles are all important to team performance, and he argued that if a balance is established, the team can achieve more successful outputs. Since Belbin linked these team roles to personality, he also developed a psychometric test to determine preferred team types. Each person has a primary and secondary preference. Belbin emphasized that in some circumstances, some roles are more important than others. Since focus teams designed for creative work usually consist of a minimum of seven and a maximum of twelve people, role combining or sharing is going to be necessary.

Nevertheless, it is worthwhile starting our consideration of team roles with the types which Belbin identified.

- *The chair (or facilitator)* – helps the team to focus, to find out what their priorities are, to develop more ideas, and to resolve conflicts. He guides and co-ordinates. He is a good communicator who has the qualities which will earn him respect from other team members. (The use of the masculine pronoun in this list of roles is for convenience only and is not intended to suggest any exclusion of female team members.)

- *The shaper* – is an energetic person who wants to make things happen. His value to the team is that he will enthusiastically promote the work of the team throughout the company. However, a shaper will probably be frustrated by the vagueness and ambiguity required in creative work. This is a role which the team builder may prefer to drop.

- *The Plant* – is imaginative, intelligent, and full of original ideas. He is also especially sensitive to criticism and apt to 'turn off' from time to time. Nevertheless, a plant (or several) in a creative team is vital. The chair has to take special care to keep them interested and ensure only constructive criticism is applied, and in the right places (see ground rules).

- *Monitor/evaluator* – is an analyst, able to gather, collate, interpret and evaluate information. He will constantly remind the rest of the team of its objectives.

- *The company worker* – is an organizer who concentrates on feasibility and ensuring a disciplined action plan.

- *The resource investigator* – is someone who can find people to help, and a detective who can find things out. This role might usefully be combined with something else, such as team worker.

- *The team worker* – is loyal to the team and a mediator. He listens to the ideas of others and builds on them. This is a very important role in a creative team.

- *The finisher* – is a progress chaser. He is keen on deadlines, and wants to keep the team on track, which can lead to impatience. This role might easily be combined with the company worker.

Belbin's team types have proved very helpful to managers building project teams, but it should not be a straightjacket. It is at its most useful in reminding us to avoid sameness in teams, such as twelve 'ideas people' or twelve analysts, or twelve 'go-getters'.

One final point on team composition – creative teams need to be volunteers. Members may be head-hunted perhaps, but it is pointless to force someone who feels intimidated by open thinking to take part in it. We might think it will be his or her loss, but we can only guess at the sort of reasons why some people are unnerved by abstraction and uncertainty. It would be unfair to such people and the rest of the team to try and persuade them to take part if the prospect did not immediately excite them.

The XYZ+20 project team

The project team is the idea of the Managing Director and he intends to act as sponsor for its work, but does not want to be directly involved. He chooses his team as follows:

- Marketing Manager;
- a production engineer;

- Purchasing Manager;

- Company Accountant;

- a skilled cabinet maker who is active in the union;

- an upholsterer;

- a secretary;

- a canteen worker;

- a retired former manager of a department store (the store is one of XYZ's key accounts).

We can see straightaway that the Managing Director of XYZ Ltd incorporates professional diversity. Although XYZ is not global, he tries to accommodate cultural diversity too:

- the production engineer is second generation Ukrainian;

- the accountant was born in Bangladesh;

- the secretary is Irish;

- the canteen worker is a Spanish student;

- the former customer is a wheelchair user.

The secretary, canteen worker and cabinet maker bring youthful enthusiasm to the team, the upholsterer, Purchasing Manager and former customer bring the wisdom of age. Four team members are women – the Marketing Manager, the secretary, the canteen worker/student and the former customer.

In terms of diversity of interests, the Managing Director establishes the following:

- the Marketing Manager is a workaholic;

- the production engineer loves science fiction;

- the Purchasing Manager plays golf and paints water-colours;

- the Company Accountant devotes all his spare time to his family;

- the skilled cabinet maker who is active in the union is also active in local politics and plays football for a pub team;

- the upholsterer is a local chess champion;

- the secretary helps to run a local youth club;

- the canteen worker is a keen dancer;

- the retired former manager of a department store is keen on theatre.

The MD decides not to apply psychometric testing, but discusses team roles with team members and the following emerges:

- The Company Accountant is suggested by other team members as the best facilitator, and he is keen to take on the role.

- Everyone agrees to 'do their own bit' to promote the work of the team throughout the company.

- The production engineer, Purchasing Manager, upholsterer and the former customer all see themselves as 'ideas' people.

- The canteen worker/student is keen to take on the role of analyst.

- The secretary is a popular person in the company and considered ideal as a resource investigator.

- The Marketing Manager feels that the output will be critical to her job and volunteers to be company worker-cum-finisher.

- The cabinet maker offers to try very hard to fulfil the role of team worker.

Briefing a team

The team will be asked to produce a 20–30 year outlook for the company, and to suggest ways in which aspects of that future outlook can be brought forward into the intermediate strategic plan (3–5 years.) The team is to produce a view of the future which can generate a shared mission for everyone in the company. A mission which is not just well-chosen words, but creates a credible, attractive picture in people's minds, something worth working for, something which will affect their behaviour. Evangelists have to start with something people could want, from shopfloor to top floor. Something which can easily be remembered, and something which people can see progress towards.

Although the team will be encouraged to be creative, creativity does not mean anarchy or chaos. Team members must understand the ground rules that are to operate. The chair/facilitator will be responsible for making sure that they do operate.

Ground rules

- *Appropriate use of judgement* – first and foremost, judgement should be suspended in idea generation exercises, and applied constructively in sessions with an analytical and evaluation purpose. (The chair could provide small cards coloured red on one side and green on the other. Participants display the green side when they are happy that the meeting is progressing well. They should switch to red if the meeting assumes a negative tone.)

- *Stretch your mind and take risks.*

- *Listen to, and expand upon the ideas of others* – No 'yes, but' – 'yes and' is required!

- *Keep objectives in mind* – Remember what you are there for – to define a prosperous future for the organization.

- *No killer phrases* – Killer phrases, such as:
  - 'thank you for that pure conjecture'
  - 'that's crazy'
  - 'we tried that before, it didn't work'
  are forbidden, and should instantly receive a red card.

- *Help each other over performance barriers* – The project is not a competition for promotion, the team will be judged on its collective output so it is in everybody's interests to provide mutual support.

The team must also be advised about the characteristics of creative teams and encouraged to pursue them.

Support from senior management

The next thing a team needs in order to perform is a 'big game' atmosphere. The Apollo mission inspired average groups to excel, a war effort has the same effect. The team needs to believe that there is something at stake. Their end result must be important.

Therefore, the focus team working on seizing the future must have sponsorship, perhaps even mentoring, from the very top of the organization, as in XYZ's case. It would be far too risky for senior management to apply a 'sink or swim' philosophy to this topic.

Independence

The team must not be constrained by day-to-day concerns whilst they are doing creative work. Many companies physically isolate their creative project teams from the office and all forms of communication with it (mobile phones must be switched off).

In the late 1980s, as recession loomed in the UK, Midland Bank's Project Raincloud team isolated themselves from the bureaucracy and the day-to-day struggles of the bank to think about the future of banking, and developed the concept of a telebanking subsidiary which was an instant success.

Feedback and reward

Creative teams need to invite their senior management sponsor occasionally to check that they are moving in the right direction. He or she has to be accessible to the team, making time to listen, review and apply constructive comment.

Resources

The team will need resources, primarily information. There should be no barriers to any member of the team gaining access to the data or views they require.

Permission to practice

In football, an inherent appreciation of who is in the best position to score the goal looks fantastically easy to the spectator – it actually takes hours and hours of practice for the team members. Practice time must encompass the freedom to treat mistakes as stepping stones.

On flights between the Earth and the Moon, Apollo spaceships were off course more than 90 per cent of the time. The crew had to repeatedly correct the trajectory, but it did not impede the overall success of the mission.

Taking people out of their regular jobs, throwing them into a team and expecting creative work is not the most productive approach, although I pay tribute to the innumerable individuals who are put into this position and succeed. Many companies find that a short period of preparation can be useful in reducing wasted effort when the project is underway.

Individual preparation

Curiosity is one of the permanent and certain characteristics of a vigorous intellect.

Samuel Johnson

Discovery consists of seeing what everyone has seen and thinking what nobody has thought.

Anon

Every individual is a marvel of unknown and unrealized possibilities.

Goethe

A number of companies prepare staff for creative work by sending them on an unusual seminar or trip to experience something new. Square, a Japanese video games company, send staff travelling the world to experience for themselves the sort of castles, forests and caves where video games could be set. Shiseido does something more random, it sends its people on seminars on everything from gymnastics to voluntary medical service in Zaire.

If time and money are not available for such luxuries, and it is considered appropriate to help members of a creative team to accommodate unusual inputs – they might be asked to read science fiction or books on unusual hobbies.

Creativity can also be enhanced if team members do spend time on solitary and speculative thinking. Some companies with outstanding records for innovation set thinking time targets for all employees because we have to be forced to meet such expectations – naturally, we prefer to do rather than think. Some companies believe it is appropriate to teach meditation, Tai Chi, or something similar.

Thinking will always give you a reward, though not always what you expected.

Lord Roy Thomson of Fleet, Canadian entrepreneur

It may also be helpful to give team members practice in trying to encourage others to think, such as running free-thinking sessions at team briefs.

Last, but not least, team members must have the opportunity to investigate whatever they feel is useful information or opinions for the project's success, such as information about the company's history, customer satisfaction surveys, etc.

Team building exercises

There is no point in sending employees to army-style boot camps complete with bullying sergeant-majors if you want creativity. Since this type of team building was intended to instil blind obedience, its relevance to creative work is limited. The sort of discipline required in creative teams is rooted in a framework for self-discipline, not subservience to external discipline.

There are some outdoor based exercises which can be creative. One of my clients described 'The Labyrinth', based at a stately home in Warwickshire. The exercises included racing in two teams on skis made for ten people and solving a problem by building a ramp and rolling a heavy barrel to the end of it. The team were also blindfolded, and then had to find out how to put balls into a pit in the order of the colours of the rainbow. They climbed on bales of hay – to set up pulleys in the trees – in order to winch up a heavy block – to get the code for a safe – without triggering a man-trap– and so on!

General team based games such as volleyball or baseball can also help the team to find out more about each other's strengths and weaknesses and working styles. But team building does not have to involve something physical. In the case of the XYZ+20 team, they have the responsibility of involving a wheelchair user in their team building. Team members could introduce themselves at length by presenting to each other on special interests, or the unusual seminar or trip they have undertaken as part of their individual preparation. There are also some ice-breaking games which are non-physical. A favourite of mine is the egg game.

The egg game
Split the team into pairs or threes. Provide these mini-teams with several eggs, and a few basic items of stationery, such as scissors, paper, string and clingfilm. Their challenge is to design a wrapping

which will protect it from at least a twelve foot drop (four metres). The mini-teams will have a time limit of two hours and a cost limit, which is at the facilitator's discretion. Having designed a successful solution, if the mini-team has time they should 'de-engineer' it to reduce cost and complexity. At the end of the two hours, the mini-teams will demonstrate their solutions and then exchange notes with each other to determine a preferred solution.

Another option, if time is available, is for the team to put on a short play or revue. In the arts, each production of a familiar play, such as a Shakespeare play, has to be new and exciting to attract audiences who are already familiar with the story. With deep professionalism, a pride and loyalty in themselves as a cast and a passion all organizations are likely to envy, the production team takes a new approach, and rehearses until they believe they can create the effect they want! The facilitator could find a familiar scene from a familiar play for two sub-teams to develop, rehearse and perform to each other in a limited timeframe, such as half a day.

The team could then move into more controversial territory, thinking through, but NOT debating, 'right–right' dilemmas or 'wrong–wrong' dilemmas. Such as:

- Should a drug which has caused many tragic birth defects, but has also been found effective in relieving suffering in an incurable disease, be licensed?

- Should banks defend customers' confidentiality at all costs, or should they pro-actively co-operate with the police or tax authorities over even small misdemeanours?

Or the team might prefer to discuss views relevant to their task, such as:

If a man will begin with certainties, he shall end in doubts; but if he will be content to begin with doubts, he shall end in certainties.
Francis Bacon (1561–1626), author of Proficiency and Advancement of
Learning

The XYZ+20 team discusses preparation with their sponsor, and decide on the following programme:

Five members volunteer to read science fiction books with elements of prophesy about the next millennium. Four, including the sci-fi hobbyist, volunteer to read about other people's hobbies. They also decide to explore each other's thinking styles by holding a mini-league within the team for a simple board game. For team building, they opt to spend a day on developing a spoof episode of a popular soap opera, set in 2020, and to be performed for colleagues in the canteen the following lunchtime. They will de-brief from the performance, with reference to the Bacon quote.

After all that, they expect to be eager and ready for the next step in the planning process.

SUMMARY

This chapter has explored the way in which a creative team can be chosen and developed to take on the project of seizing the future for the business.

- Creative work is a social, not a solitary activity.

- A creative team is the complete opposite of an adversarial 'political' committee.

- Ideas can be drawn from the widest team possible – the company and all its stakeholders.

- The focus team should be drawn from diverse professions, cultures and interests.

- Team roles should be assumed by team members, to ensure that all necessary activities are covered.

- The team needs to be given the right framework and support for its work, including the time to prepare as individuals and as a team, for the task in hand.

Chapter 4 explains the work involved for the team in building a thorough picture of the 'now' situation of the business.

Analysing today

Identifying the present position

An easy start to the process of seizing the future is to explore the team's collective knowledge of the situation our organization finds itself in today. Or is it so easy? Many planning teams start this step full of confidence, only to discover gaps in what they need to know, and/or that they have far too much data which is of questionable value. Nevertheless, the process can still be started with a few basic items of 'tombstone' data, which state where the company stands. Most plans contain a few recent historical figures and a statistical trend. These are relevant things to note, discuss and park. A performance chart, of the format illustrated in Table 4.1, can be completed and the figures will say something about the company as a going concern.

What business are we in?

Although it sounds like a philosophical minefield, the next question to ask ourselves is 'why does our organization exist?' What customer needs do we fulfil and therefore what business are we in? The answer does not have to be very detailed. We have already discussed companies which have seen themselves in a product business rather than in the role of fulfilling customer needs, and have therefore lost their hegemony.

Microsoft had an avowed intent to write the software to put a computer on every desk and in every home. So, from the early 1980s, everyone knew that Microsoft wanted to make computing as

TABLE 4.1 Key performance trends – recent past

	$T-3$	$T-2$	$T-1$	This year's Plan	Trend
Sales volume					
Sales revenue					
Market share					
Gross margin					
Operating profit					
Capital employed					
Return on capital employed					
Stock turnover					
Debtor days					
Liquidity ratio					
People employed					

popular as television, even when there was widespread disbelief that computers would ever be commonplace.

Glaxo states that man's greatest enemy is disease and the greatest enemy of disease is Glaxo, so everyone knows that Glaxo wants to find new cures.

Can we be so succinct about what our organization wants to do for the world? All we need to establish is what we believe that we help our customers to achieve, and that should tell us a few things about what sort of organization we are. If there seems to be a mismatch, or the 'reason for being' is not defined or does not seem good enough, then it would be the first indicator of something that must be done in order to seize the future. However, we do not need to find solutions at this stage, merely note our deliberations. It is said that the essence of intelligence lies in being able to not respond immediately to anything and everything we find.

What business environment/s do we operate in?

Now we have established the very core of our identity, we probably have some great ideas about what we should be doing. If these ideas come out in discussion they should be captured, but we cannot do anything with them just yet. Once again, we have to pause. No organization is an island, we are operating in a business environment, or several. We are affected by laws, economic cycles, social trends, technological change and even the weather, and other external impacts which cannot be controlled, such as sporting successes or major tragedies.

Of course, for seizing the future we cannot take into account one-off events. But we can acknowledge everyday impacts. Huge mistakes can be made if we fail to analyse the business environment, and the opportunities and threats inherent within it.

It ought to be very easy to do. Information about the business environment is very much in the public domain. The only cost involved is the time involved in gathering it and analysing it. The answers to all the following questions can usually be found out from seeking and applying to our circumstances, information available in most countries from government departments, research institutes, consumer associations and industry watchers:

- What policies and legislation affect us?

- How does the state of the economy affect our business?

- How do demographics affect us?

- What do social trends mean for our business?

- How much can technology do to us and for us?

- What other external impacts do we need to monitor (e.g. weather)?

Policies and legislation

All organizations are affected by initiatives taken by politicians to govern the world of work and transfer of goods and services. Some people argue, particularly in Western Europe, but also in the USA, that there is too much legislation, too much 'red tape' and that it stifles enterprise. Occasionally, the law is an ass, but most laws exist for good reasons and business people are proud to demonstrate their compliance. In any event, would any company seriously want to be seen lobbying their government to repeal health and safety at work legislation or consumer protection legislation? It would not make for very good public relations.

The sorts of laws which we have to work with may be divided into five categories:

- *To protect shareholders/stockholders:*
  - fiduciary duties of directors, and directors' duty of care
  - company law

- *To protect employees:*
  - health and safety
  - equal opportunities
  - employment law, governing individuals' rights at work (e.g. against unfair dismissal)

- *To protect customers:*
  - consumer protection
  - professional liability insurance

- *To protect the community in which we operate:*
  - tax and duties
  - planning regulations (use of land, premises, etc.)
  - public liability insurance
  - environmental regulations

- *To protect suppliers:*
  - copyright
  - contract law

From the way I have set out this list, it should be evident that the stakeholder society has been with us for sometime. The laws of most mature economies ensures that companies pay due regard to stake-holders' interests. Most of these laws are business as usual, and whilst they need to be understood and complied with, they are not going to shape the future of the company.

Of course, we cannot all be lucky enough to work for companies with uncontroversial products, like paper clips, unlikely to attract the lobbyists' or legislators'eye. Some laws are very specific in their effect on particular industries:

- privacy laws – the media;

- cold-calling regulation – telemarketing agencies;

- environmental laws – energy companies;

- shopping hours – retail;

- pension mis-selling – financial services;

- land use – construction and associated trades;

- prohibition/legalization of substances – pharmaceutical, food and drink.

Parliaments are full of ex-lawyers, and therefore new laws are a fact of life. If our trading activities are bringing old ladies as well as young radicals out on to the streets in protest today, we can be pretty sure they will be illegal at some stage in the future. At this stage in the construction of our future outlook, we need only to note current law relating specifically to our industry and markets, and also the policies of relevant political parties and interest groups who might change things in the future.

Economic cycles

For decades, the UK has seen a pattern of slumps of increasing severity at the turn of a decade, and booms in the middle years. The most accentuated boom–bust cycle was the accelerated growth of 1984–87, followed by deepening recession which was at its worst in 1990–92. All political parties are determined to stop this sort of boom–bust economics, but to date have only resided over bigger swings. The USA has similar cycles, and Asia seems to be developing them. Western Europe economies seem to change more gradually, apart from exceptional impacts, such as the re-unification of Germany.

Most companies these days operate in more than one country, and must rely on local knowledge to stay ahead of these trends and know when to plan for growth and when to batten down the hatches and make sure costs are under control. The last recession in the UK triggered widespread 'downsizing'. Many people who were affected by downsizing ruefully reflect that it did not stop massive bankruptcies, and those companies that did survive were left ill-equipped to respond to recovery.

Demographics and social trends

Social trends are not just the domain of trend-conscious social scientists; they mean things for businesses. Simply tracking the impact of the baby boomer generation, the lump in the demographic charts which represents people born between 1945 and 1960, can be a successful strategy in anticipating consumer needs and leading the market in fulfilling them. Habitat, a retail phenomenon in its early years, captured the hearts and souls of the UK baby boomers who were furnishing their own homes in the 1970s.

As this demographic bulge of people who still wear jeans and listen to The Beatles approaches retirement age, many with comfortable pensions, a number of companies have set out to capture their business. The leisure industry in particular sees great opportunities, for example in the UK a travel company for the over-50s has been a huge success.

There is much debate about the nature of the 'boomer' market. Recent research suggests that the 'ageing hippies' are getting somewhat conservative in their tastes and careful about what they spend. They take much of their leisure at home, and are sceptical about information technology. The interesting angle for suppliers is that baby boomers throughout the USA and Western Europe have more in common with each other than fellow countrymen from other generations. 'Beatles and blue jeans' culture has that power.

Working with demographic patterns is relatively easy because most consumers that organizations want to know about have already been born and their governments have been gathering data about them. In retailing, it is vital to know the patterns of the catchment area of each store, by age, income, cultural origin and family size. This enables plans to be made to get the right stock to the right stores at the right time.

Understanding the attitudes of those consumers and what they are interested in, as we saw in the 'boomer' example, is more subjective. Nevertheless, some things can be monitored which can provide clues about changing attitudes. It would be fairly easy in most countries to find statistics on the following:

- The number of people living together as households, which indicates (over time) changing attitudes to family values.

- The number of people with cars, which indicates (over time) levels of mobility.

- The number of people with home computers, which indicates whether 'technophilia' is overcoming 'technophobia'.

- The number of people using recycling centres, which indicates concern for the environment.

- The number of people with heart problems, which indicates attitudes to diet, exercise, etc.

In addition to noting how government statistics have changed in recent years, it is also said that a social trend can be identified by tracking over time the number of column inches devoted to it in popular newspapers. One thing is sure, we are never really sure that a trend is a trend until it has moved consistently in one direction for many years. As we shall see with the analogy of stock market history in the next chapter, we also have to make judgements about when trends are likely to kick back on themselves.

Attitudes to consumption itself are critical, as green pressure groups make symbolic gestures such as opening 'non-shops'.

When we progress to talking about seizing the future, we will see that it is children's attitudes which can be especially interesting. For the time being, finding out current trends is challenge enough, and noting whether or not our company is in line with them or behind them.

Technology

Technological changes ought to be keeping all business people awake at night. As more and more people around the world sign up to the Internet, how we use technology will make or break us. Of course, technology rarely takes off as quickly as technologists might wish. Because I worked for IBM in the 1980s, for most of that decade I enjoyed the luxuries of e-mail for communicating with colleagues and tele-working. So, it is a bit difficult to comprehend why these productivity enhancers are still in their growth phase in 1997, whilst mobile phones have become commonplace.

Perhaps the Internet needs to become much more usable, but even in its present state, it cannot be ignored. For the purpose of our long-term planning, all we need to note for now is:

- What technology is available (in general and specific to our business)?

- What are we using?

- What is the gap?

If ideas arise about how to close the gap, capture them for future use.

Other external impacts

Increasingly clients are demanding that the weather, in particular, appears on the business environment list. For example, energy companies are worried about the effects of global warming on their profitability, and clothing retailers need to change their seasons and clothing ranges according to changes in weather patterns. Weather forecasting is still an imprecise science, but there is some consensus at least about the types of weather conditions and degree of volatility which might have to be accommodated in any particular region of the world.

We need to note our awareness of this and other external effects and our readiness to respond.

The acid test – what is actionable?

It is very interesting to take a look at life, the universe and everything which might change the nature of our business. At the end of the exercise however, we need to make a summary of what, out of everything we have looked at, is actionable. Table 4.2 summarizes the review of the current business environment undertaken by the project team in our XYZ+20 example, giving them some food for thought at this early stage.

How is the market structured?

The team needs to move on to analyse the structure of the markets in which the company operates. Who adds what value, and where are they in the supply chain? Where is the power in the supply chain? Are there any external or abstract influencers? Who controls information about the end-consumers? How fierce is the competition? Who are the competitors now and what are their strengths and weaknesses compared to ours? Is it easy for others to enter the market, or for consumers to find substitutes? Is it possible for links in the value chain to be skipped or reconfigured?

The first exercise is to describe the market of today. This is best achieved by drawing it as a map of the flow of value. The example given in Figure 4.1 is a generic starting point. You would need to configure your own, as shown in Figure 4.2, which is for our furniture manufacturer, XYZ Ltd.

In Figure 4.2, we can see that percentages have been added to show where there is choice in terms of a route to market and how it is split. It is most important at this stage to map the whole market. If you just concentrate on your portion of it, you run the risk of failing to appreciate how the dynamics of other forces in the market could impact on your

TABLE 4.2 Furniture manufacturing – summary of major actionable trends in the business environment

Topic	Item	Gap?
Politics/ legislation	The major industry-specific regulations are concerned with consumer safety, e.g. fire resistant materials	XYZ has always complied with minimum legislative requirements, but has never been ahead of the trends. There is a need to consult with safety lobby groups to ensure we are ready for the next step.
Economic cycles	Currently in recession	Since the recession of the early 1980s, XYZ has established enough flexibility to be able to minimize stockholding, lay off staff, etc. in a crisis. Readiness for recovery is more fragile and needs more work. How do we expand quickly when the indicators are optimistic?
Social trends	Demographics	If baby boomers are really becoming more conservative it is great news for XYZ as they will buy our classical range. However, dominance of the industry seems to depend on capturing the imagination of the generation setting up home for the first time, which XYZ has never done.
Social trends	Environmental concerns	We have a relatively good image, although not all materials used are recyclable. We do sponsor charities who distribute used furniture to people in need.
Technology changes	Buying furniture over the Internet	Yes! No idea how, or whether to respond at this stage.
	Manufacturing technology	XYZ has never been at the forefront of new production techniques or new raw materials. We could develop more knowledge and be better prepared.
Other	Warmer weather leading to demand for outdoor and conservatory furniture	XYZ didn't see it coming and was completely left behind.

FIGURE 4.1   Flow of value map – generic

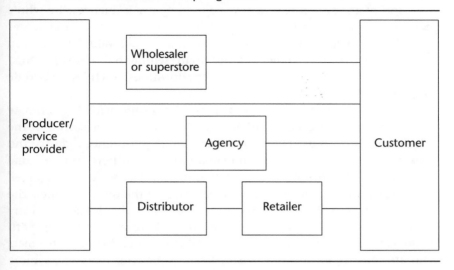

FIGURE 4.2   Flow of value map – XYZ Furniture

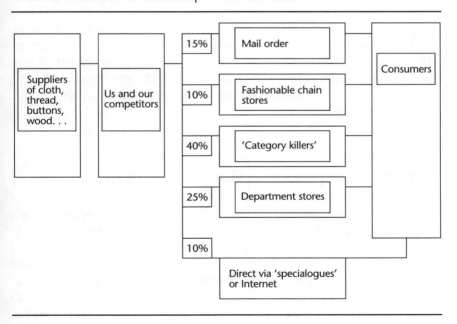

part. Indeed, the team must establish how these other players in the market affect the customer's experience of the XYZ product.

You might also consider how your company influences the whole picture. How do you work with distributors and retailers to add value? How do you work 'upstream' with suppliers to add value? Could you market directly to customers rather than selling on to distributors/retailers? Technology can offer new opportunities, such as electronic shopping.

A manufacturer's desire to own its relationship with the ultimate consumer is not necessarily unfair or destructive to other parties in the value chain. Brokers used to be all powerful in the insurance industry and consumers relied on their recommendation. Then a new entrant came into the market – insurers who wanted direct contact with the customer. This caused some panic, until it was realized that the only customers the direct insurers were interested in were low risk ones who did not need any advice. Brokers can now concentrate on working in partnership with insurance companies to mutually add value and provide for consumers who are looking for a more personal service or who represent a more unusual risk.

One factor which we have not shown in Figures 4.1 and 4.2, but which needs to be considered, are the hidden forces in market maps. Who exerts influence in the market? Industry associations vary in their power over members. The most powerful associations need to be closely understood. We must also consider gatekeepers, the people or organizations who might stop things happening in the market. For example, utility companies have to abide by regulations made by regulators (e.g. Oftel in telecommunications), and in the USA, the Food and Drug Administration very carefully vets any new products from the pharmaceutical and food industries.

Where is the power in the market map?

It is not enough to describe the market, we also have to consider where power lies in the market, and the analysis tool most commonly applied to this task is Michael Porter's Five Forces (Porter, 1980). One way of estimating how much pressure there will be on your prices and profitability is to examine competitive forces in the market.

The five forces and the relationships between them are illustrated in Figure 4.3. Consider each of the five forces and how they affect the market in which you operate.

FIGURE 4.3   The five forces of power in the market. From Porter (1980).

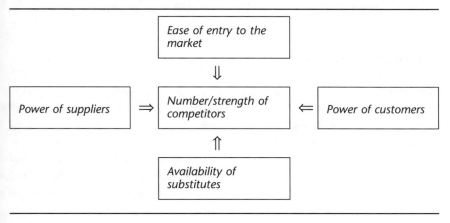

Ease of entry to the market

Does it require huge capital investment to produce these products/ services to fulfil these customer needs, or can anyone set up in their garage? If it is easy to enter the market, count this competitive pressure as HIGH. If the only feasible entrant would be an eccentric multi-million- aire, count it as LOW.

Power of suppliers

Are there only a few suppliers of the raw materials you need? If so, this competitive pressure is HIGH. If you can get supplies anywhere, it is LOW.

Porter's model seems to assume that multi-sourcing is a good thing, but in many industries, better quality and lower costs can be achieved by single-sourcing partnerships with a chosen supplier for strategic products (such as raw materials) and some services. This would diffuse any perceived competitive pressure from suppliers. It is more pertinent in the 1990s to ask whether or not your suppliers can leapfrog you and sell directly to the end customer. If they can, then competitive pressure from suppliers is HIGH.

Number and strength of competitors

If you are the brand leader and your competitors simply follow your lead, this competitive pressure is LOW. If there are lots of healthy companies vying for brand leadership, the pressure is HIGH. What you need to know in detail about your competitors is discussed later in this chapter.

Power of customers

You may have a small number of big accounts, in which case customer power is HIGH, as it would be a very serious matter if you were to lose any one of them. It used to be assumed that if you were selling to millions of consumers, then customer power was LOW – not any more! A significant minority of those millions of consumers will be knowledgeable and organized enough to exert power in the marketplace, especially via consumers associations and consumer programmes in the media.

Innumerable academic and industry studies in the past few years indicate that mature markets, the internationalization of supply chains and the increasing sophistication of the consumer are all leading to a situation in which consumer power is universally high.

Availability of substitutes

If the price of coffee is high, people may drink tea instead. If there are a high number of substitutes for your product, this competitive pressure is HIGH. If your offering is unique, it is LOW. Regard the option to do nothing as a substitute too, it is often a tempting one for the customer!

Theoretically, if you have three or more 'HIGH' forces then your profits are under pressure. There are few industries where this does not apply which is why there is an emphasis in modern business theory on 'diffusing' competitive pressure. This is achieved through methods such as partnerships with suppliers and big customers, creating relational barriers to entry, acquiring or inventing the substitutes and loyalty marketing. However, at this stage of the team process, we are just noting our challenges. Potential solutions can be collated for later use.

In the case of XYZ, the picture which emerges is captured in Figure 4.4.

Two high and two medium competitive pressures indicates difficult circumstances for XYZ and the need for some kind of significant innovation to break the trap of low profitability which is probably inherent in the market.

FIGURE 4.4   The five forces of power and XYZ Furniture

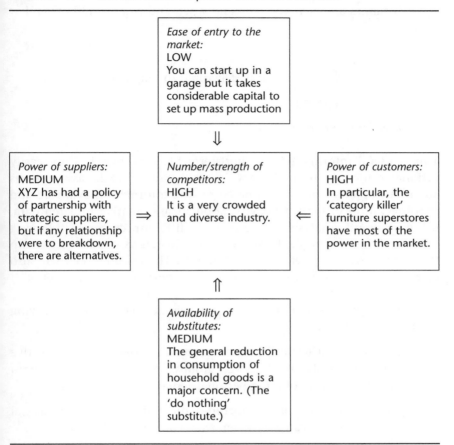

Segmenting the value stages in the market map

Customers are not an amorphous mass, but individuals with differing lifestyles and tastes. This means that we need to analyse a different dimension of the market map as well. Intuitively, we know that there are groups of customers, whose buying behaviour is determined by income, mobility and taste. How can we know how the market breaks up into segments? To understand this might be helpful in analysing which way the market is going to move in the future.

I have six honest serving men, they serve me well and true,
Their names are what and why and when and where and how and
who.

Rudyard Kipling

Usually, company information is structured to tell us the following:

■   what customers buy,

■   when/how/where or from whom.

This is useful information for short-term logistics, but it is not easily
actionable for long-term strategy. We will have to make assumptions
about customer segmentation based on the information available and
on observation of market activity. Sophisticated market research data,
using trade-off analysis to determine different customers' buying
criteria, if they are available, would show clusters as in Table 4.3. From
the clusters, you can define your segments. The research data will also
give you some indication of the relative proportion of the market each
segment fills.

The Segments A–F in Table 4.3 are defined by their buying
behaviour as follows:

■   *Segment A* – 'Classical' buyers: reasonably well-off, conservative
people, probably in older age groups, most likely to buy from
department stores offering personal service.

■   *Segment B* – People on low incomes, most likely to look for special
offers in the big 'category killer' stores or shop in the sales.

■   *Segment C* – People driven by practicalities, may have boisterous
children or pets!

■   *Segment D* – Aspiring people.

■   *Segment E* – Fashion conscious people, probably young people.

■   *Segment F* – Lifestyle driven people – identification with a particular
brand says something about the way they live their lives.
Specialogues are likely to appeal to them.

It would be difficult to serve the whole market excellently. We ought to
make judgements about what sort of market segments or accounts are
most attractive to our business. Where should we be concentrating our
resources? We need to establish criteria for 'attractiveness', set priorities
for them, and then score each segment or account accordingly. An

TABLE 4.3 Customer segmentation for the current furniture market

Customers' buying criteria	Segment A (25%)	Segment B (20%)	Segment C (15%)	Segment D (20%)	Segment E (10%)	Segment F (10%)
Price	10	60	40	20	30	0
Quality	25	20	40	30	10	30
Style	25	20	0	20	40	20
Brand values	10	0	10	20	20	40
Service from sales staff	30	0	10	0	0	10
Totals	100%	100%	100%	100%	100%	100%

Critical success factor analysis, based on input to the GE/McKinsey Directional Policy Matrix, as illustrated in McDonald (1984).

example for Segments A–C is given in Table 4.4. Similar analysis can be carried out for each segments of the market.

Obviously most businesses are interested in the customers who will pay extra for quality, brand values or lifestyle attributes. Yet we can see, from this brief look at the world that our furniture manufacturer has to deal with, that there are good reasons for fulfilling the needs of other niche markets as well.

So we have half the story. The other half involves the customers' perceptions of how particular brands fulfil their needs. Of course there are complications, for example, in the case of segment A who heavily weight

TABLE 4.4 Attractiveness factors – Segments A–C

Customer attractiveness factors	Weight	Score, Seg A	Score × Weight	Score, Seg B	Score × Weight	Score, Seg C	Score × Weight
Size of market	20	8	160	7	140	6	120
Growth of market	50	3	150	3	150	6	300
Profitability	30	5	150	2	60	6	180
Totals	100%		460		400		600

Market attractiveness factor analysis, based on input to the GE/McKinsey Directional Policy Matrix, as illustrated in McDonald (1984).

the service from sales staff. Since that is something the manufacturer cannot influence, weights have had to be redistributed accordingly.

Why do they/don't they buy from us?

Table 4.5 shows a critical factor analysis of XYZ and two of its competitors, ASY and WQR, for Segment A of the customer market. ASY is clearly the best as far as this segment is concerned because of its quality leadership, although WQR has the best positioning for style. The scores that customers have assigned to our example company indicate that they might be attracted to it if times were hard and they needed a good price. However, we can tell from the weightings that price is not a main driver for these customers.

There are good reasons why XYZ should maintain its position in this segment, not least because the company has a presence already, and it is the biggest segment in the market. But where else must XYZ be? Combining the market attractiveness factors and critical success factors together in a matrix gives us the actionable picture shown in Figure 4.5 of their position in their market today.

The map in Figure 4.5 actually shows quite a dangerous outlook for XYZ. Although it has historically been a 'classics' company, XYZ is not particularly strong in this segment. The company is most popular with bargain-hunters, who are the second least attractive segment. The company looks good in the 'practicals' segment, but it clearly has a very weak position in the two most attractive segments.

TABLE 4.5   Buying criteria – XYZ and its competitors (Segment A)

Segment A Customers' buying criteria	Weight	Score, XYZ	Score × Weight	Score, WQR	Score × Weight	Score, ASY	Score × Weight
Price	15	8	120	4	60	7	105
Quality	35	6	210	4	140	8	280
Style	35	5	175	7	245	3	105
Brand values	15	3	45	7	105	8	120
Totals	100%		550		550		610

Critical success factor analysis, based on input to the GE/McKinsey Directional Policy Matrix, as illustrated in McDonald (1984).

FIGURE 4.5 Attractiveness vs. performance matrix.
Note that the vertical axis runs from right to left. This may seem counter-intuitive, but it is the way the original designers intended it to be. Our focus is concentrated on the top left-hand box. This box is based on the Directional Policy Matrix jointly developed by General Electric and McKinsey, as illustrated in McDonald (1984).

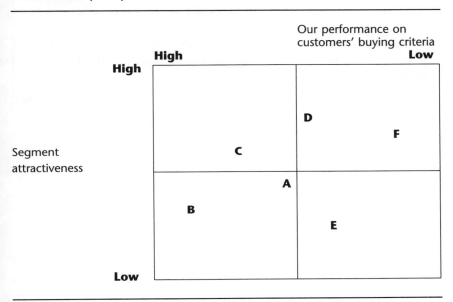

A textbook response to this analysis would be to hold steady in Segment B, invest moderately to avoid decline in A, invest in C and D, experiment with F and drop E. However, the XYZ+20 team are temporarily going to put this map to one side, because the 20 year outlook may demand alternative approaches.

Now our 'market audit' of the present situation is complete. Next we have to ask ourselves – how did we get here?

SUMMARY

In this chapter, we have established:

- what we are like as a going concern;
- what business we are in;

- what aspects of the business environment affect us;

- the structure of the market;

- where power lies in the market

- which segments of the market are most attractive to us;

- the relative strengths and weaknesses we have in those segments.

In Chapter 5, we discuss what we can learn from history, including the history of our industry and our business, which should inform our expectations of the future.

CHAPTER FIVE

Learning from history

Study the past, if you would divine the future.

Confucius

Hegel was right when he said that we learn from history that men never learn anything from history.

George Bernard Shaw

When you look at when the seeds were sown for our most successful products of the last two or three years – for example in mobile phones and digital switching – it was 20 or even 25 years ago.

Jorma Ollila, Chief Executive of Nokia

The importance of the past

I am indebted to Hugh Marlow for introducing me to the simple truth recognized since ancient times, that if we can find an historical analogy for a current situation and we analyse what happened in the past, we can make reasonable assumptions about the future. Regrettably, when I ask at workshops and conferences if anyone feels confident that they understand the history of their companies, nobody raises their hand.

Even at quite senior levels, few people know about the history of the organization whose future is in their hands, or the industry in which they are working. Business history in not widely taught, business schools tend to look at individual cases rather than developments over decades. Even history in general is a blur to many business decision makers. We believe that we learn by mistakes, but life would be much easier if we learnt by other people's mistakes, be they those of Napoleon or the Chief Executive's grandfather's first competitor. An understanding of company, industry and business history is something the planning team need to develop before progressing to scenario building. This is something more than the case studies offered in business books – it involves placing events in very wide contexts.

Within the exercise, the process involves an in-depth review of what the business environment was like in the distant past (20–30 years ago), what needs were being fulfilled by our company or its predecessors, and what the market structure was like. Consideration is then given to what trends over the past 20 years will continue on their steady course, what is cyclical and may return, what may stop and what may go into reverse. Foresight relies on a lot of hindsight. Sometimes the strongest message I leave with clients is that there is nothing new under the sun, and if we can only take time to think about re-using the successful solutions of the past or avoiding the mistakes of the past then we have no need for concern.

Example – Stock market history

Stock market historian David Schwartz correctly predicted the stock market slump in October 1997, which occurred almost exactly 10 years after the crash of 1987. He also predicted that it would not be as severe, but neither was it likely to be a 'minnow' (small drop). He was able to make this prediction based on detailed studies, going back 80 years, of the factors in the business environment causing market fluctuations.

In a broader historical perspective, there was nothing special about the 1987 and 1997 drops in the value of UK shares, apart from the speed of the drops, caused of course by ever-improving technology. (Corrections also happened very speedily, especially in 1997.)

Schwartz had identified that each 'mega-drop' in UK share prices since 1918, bar one, had been precipitated by three identical problems:

- the economy being in recession or about to be in recession;

- shocking political or social events perceived to undermine the stability of values and institutions;

- highly abnormal retail price increases or decreases.

This was particularly noticeable in the great depression of 1928–32. Boom in the USA led to recession in the UK before Wall Street crashed in 1929. Extremist politics, fascism and communism, were widely feared. In 1926 there had been a crippling General Strike. Retail prices were falling dramatically. In 1997, these three factors were present in Asia where the crash was most severe.

The tragedy of stock market history is that people commit suicide, apparently unable to assimilate that crashes reverse only small parts of the long rallies which precede them. The philosophical traders start buying again. They buy cheap, the market rallies again and delivers their profits.

Example – the effect of world events on business

Hugh Marlow's (1994) holistic model for forecasting is best explained through one of its most notable successes, the prediction of the outcome of the failed Russian coup in 1991. The events of the 1991 attempted coup followed a traditional pattern starting with the seizure of communication centres and immediate claims of success regardless of the real situation, which could only be guessed at in the West. Pundits rushed to predict the return of Communism and the stock markets started to wobble. Meanwhile, Marlow's client waited for his analysis, which was based on a comparison of the factors driving the 1917 revolution with the factors at play in the attempted coup.

The first factor which he considered was the geographical epicentre of the coup activity. St Petersburg had been pivotal in the 1917 revolution (and many previous changes in Russia). In 1991, coup activity was centred on Moscow, historically a more passive city.

The second factor he considered was the personalities of the coup leaders. Lenin and Trotsky, in common with most other leaders of successful change, were charismatic personalities. In 1991, the coup leaders were 'grey men'. The defender of *perestroika*, Boris Yeltsin, had more appeal.

The third factor he considered was that in 1917, the Army and Navy supported the Soviet cause. In 1991, after *perestroika* and *glasnost*, the armed forces seemed to have developed a reluctance to fire on their own people.

Marlow therefore advised that the coup would fail, and his client was able to make money whilst everyone else dashed in the other direction.

The premise of Marlow's model, as shown in Figure 5.1, is that comparison of events over time, in the context of their location, enables us to recognize similarities and dissimilarities which lead us to establish intuitively an expected outcome, with reasonable confidence in the probability of being right.

FIGURE 5.1 An holistic forecasting model. Based on Marlow (1994)

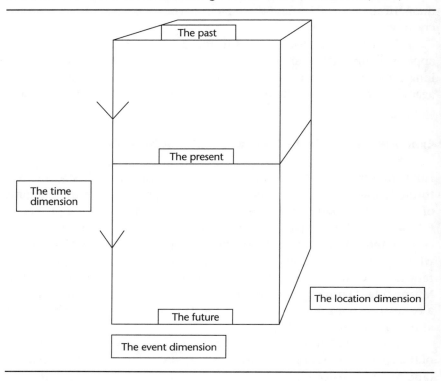

Even more probable than political history repeating itself, is the probability of patterns of business history recurring. James Utterback (1994) has examined the disturbing regularity with which leading companies, throughout industrial history, have followed their core technologies into obsolescence. He traces the historical antecedents of this tendency back to the Industrial Revolution. In the early nineteenth century, the New England ice-cutting industry built a formidable delivery business across America. In the 1860s, ice-making machines arrived from France, but the ice-cutting industry did not embrace the new technology. The industry did not even carry their natural product south in refrigerated ships.

Utterback's research revealed that radical innovations usually come from outside the industry they most affect, and they also exist for many years before they become commercially significant. For example, early personal computers were put together in garages, and the UNIX operating system came from a university source.

Building an understanding of the past

The creative team should choose a period in the past which is beyond their comfort zones. I always suggest 25–30 years. Their task is then to find out about the company, industry and markets as they were then, using the same steps as in the last chapter. If the company was not in existence 20 or 30 years ago, the team should study the market leader in the industry at that time. If the industry was not is existence 20 or 30 years ago, the team should research what preceded it. How were the needs which the company addresses being fulfilled? If the timeframe does not provide significant inspiration, dig deeper into history.

Professional institutes: craft guilds

I did a piece of work for a professional institute whose 150 year history had been one of constant expansion and success. In order to establish a 'sanity check' which introduced a perspective on their challenges for the future, I researched back 900 years to the medieval craft guilds. The craft guilds were powerful institutions throughout Europe. The earliest ones were established in the UK around 1100–35.

The objective of a craft guild was to monopolize a particular profession in a particular area (e.g. City of London), in order to fix selling prices and wage rates. Few succeeded because guild rivalry ensured a degree of competition. (This is also true of professional institutes today.) They were hierarchical and elitist institutions, with some legislative powers. (This is also true of professional institutes today.) Potential members had to prove technical competence, appropriate capital backing, and social eligibility. (Today, the emphasis is just on technical competence.)

Craft guilds declined in the sixteenth century. There were a number of contributory factors for this:

- increasing power of national governments;

- social change in some countries caused by the Reformation (emergence of merchant capitalists);

- exploration of new markets (the East, the New World);

- changes in the capital structure of businesses (e.g. the emergence of companies);

- the movement of industry from rural areas into towns.

The global economy today is characterized by changing power structures, where the kudos of being trained by a high-profile global company, known to be rigorous in their selection techniques and generous in their development of employees, presents challenges to traditional professional institutes to defend their quality branding.

Obviously, the further back you go, the more difficult it will be to find out much detail about performance, but it should still be possible to identify the forces which caused change.

We will progress through this exercise with the XYZ+20 team. We discussed the waves of change in the furniture industry in Chapter 2 (see Figure 2.5).

The team note first of all that XYZ Ltd were busy making classical furniture whilst much bigger competitors were market leaders in style. The older team members suggest this is a hidden strength – XYZ was never on a fashion roller coaster, but fulfilled the evergreen consumer need for comfort with an evergreen formula. Younger members argue that, whilst it has been a good formula for survival, it has constrained the company's ability to thrive, and the project ought to be about imagining future market leadership for XYZ.

These views are explored and parked, whilst the team dig deeper into what XYZ was like 20–30 years ago. Let's assume that 20–30 years' information is available from the company archives. First of all, it is worthwhile finding a few basic items of 'tombstone' data, which state what the company was like as a going concern (Table 5.1).

The historical picture is likely to be quite different from the review of the recent past we looked at in the last exercise. Sales and costs would look like they were on an ever-increasing spiral, but most of the increase would be due to high rates of inflation. Stock levels were higher, because information systems were not sophisticated enough to support just-in-time manufacturing. More people were employed, as manufacturing was more labour intensive and subject to union influence. Debt was even more problematic, as its value was being constantly eroded by inflation. The project team benefits from discussing why it was so different. The impact of changes in technology, employment law, customer sophistication and

TABLE 5.1   Key performance trends – distance past

	$T-25$	$T-24$	$T-23$	$T-22$	*Trend*
Sales volume					
Sales revenue					
Market share					
Gross margin					
Operating profit					
Capital employed					
Return on capital employed					
Stock turnover					
Debtor days					
Liquidity ratio					
People employed					

competitive intensity will be seen to have had their subtle effects on the financial health of the business.

What business were we in?

What customer needs were we (or the industry market leader) fulfilling? Logically, it should be the same then as now. If not, the team should discuss why not. Has the company changed direction? If so, what caused it to do so?

Our furniture example is stable enough, but what if your industry was not in existence, what else was fulfilling the needs the industry addresses now? Perhaps needs were suppressed, by some mechanism such as rationing, or the high cost of fulfilling them, or through lack of awareness of possible fulfilments. If so, what hints were there that new solutions were required?

XYZ was concentrating on comfort and practicality, core needs throughout centuries. Demographic changes meant that new consumers with new values were changing the nature of the industry. They demanded at least style and some were beginning to demand novelty. One of the catch-phrases of the time was 'and now for something completely different'.

What was the business environment like?

What laws, economic cycles, social trends, technological change or weather were affecting the market, and in what way? What were the everyday impacts? What were the opportunities and threats inherent within the business environment?

Then as now, information about the business environment would have been very much in the public domain, and a surprising amount of detail might be available via libraries or information search consultants. So we must ask ourselves as we did in our review of the present:

- What policies and legislation affected us/our industry/the market?

- How did the state of the economy affect our business/our industry/ the market?

- How did demographics affect us/our industry/the economy in general?

- What did social trends mean for our business/our industry/the economy in general?

- How much was technology doing to us and for us/our industry/the economy in general?

- What other external impacts affected us/our industry/the economy in general?

Policies and legislation

We should start to see the link between political lobbying and legislation. Laws which specifically affect our industry today may have been only a twinkle in an activist's eye many years ago. Think about what the 'health lobby' have achieved in terms of legislation, such as the banning of television tobacco advertising, the banning of drinking and driving, food labelling requirements and so on. Think about what the 'consumer lobby' has achieved in terms of the right to goods 'fit for purpose', the right to rescind unfair contracts, etc. Note how much change there has been which has specifically affected your company and your industry. Has there been incremental change over the past 30 years? Was change caused by some dramatic impact, or has political opinion on any topic completed a full circle in this time frame?

In the case of the furniture example:

- Clearly fiscal tactics to suppress consumer demand were a problem in the past, and will probably always be a challenge for this type of product. Interest rate changes in the 1990s perform the same function as tax rises and credit controls in the 1960s and 1970s.

- It was probably never imagined in the 1960s that in the 1980s laws would be introduced which severely curtailed trade union rights. No one would have planned on the hope that it would happen, but thinking about the possibility might have resulted in other ideas to achieve more flexibility in manufacturing.

- Safety was not such an important issue, but the dangers associated with wood dust in factories and foam in homes were known. Initiatives could have been taken to exceed legislative requirements and gain market advantage.

Economic cycles

Economic cycles have been with us for a long time, but the way in which companies have managed themselves through them has varied. What were the major economic impacts 20–30 years ago, and how did your company and your industry respond?

In the case of the furniture example, it is clear that the industry is very susceptible to economic cycles, and needs to have contingency plans for reducing capacity in recessions and for responding quickly to booms.

Demographics and social trends

Demographics would show then, as now, the disproportionate effect of the post-war baby boom. In terms of the sheer number of new consumers, it was good news for industry. The difficulty was understanding what these new consumers wanted. The baby boomers were rebellious teenagers in the 1960s; the youth culture of the time is frequently described as a social revolution. The hippies eventually threw away their beads and got jobs in banks, but in many ways they were still rebellious consumers in the 1970s, demanding more choice, more change and low prices.

In the case of the furniture example, the manufacturers who so adeptly picked up the suppressed demand of the growing middle classes of the late 1950s clearly suffered as a result of failing to respond to the demands of the baby boomers. It had always been assumed, until the baby boomers, that people changed their attitude to fashion as they aged. In fact, many baby boomers, who are now in their fifties, still have some 'young' attitudes.

We would of course, note dramatic differences in the social trend statistics:

- *Statistics which might be available for the 1960s and 1970s:*
  - number of people living together as households (bigger, more traditional families);
  - number of people with cars (not so many – very few two car-households);
  - number of people with heart problems (probably more).

- *And those things we measure today which were not even thought of then:*
  - number of people with home computers – zero;
  - number of people using recycling centres – zero.

As mentioned in Chapter 4, in addition to noting how the social trend statistics have changed in recent years, social trends can be identified by tracking the number of column inches devoted to them in popular newspapers. What were the big stories of the time? Also, can we get any information, apart from anecdotes of the team members' experiences, of what children's attitudes were?

Technology

The 1960s was an era inspired by the space race, but when I started work in 1972, a magnetic strip accounting machine was the height of sophistication for a medium-sized employer in a medium-sized town! In 1975 I went to work for a multinational company which had a computer which sat in the basement eating punch cards and turning them into piles of virtually incomprehensible print-out. User-friendly it was not.

There was an expectation that computers were going to become more important. Companies who did not have them aspired to them, and mini-computers were a big success when they became available in the late 1970s. If anyone in the 1970s had wished to explore where technology might go, the works of Arthur C Clarke and other top science fiction writers who had contacts with the elite scientific research laboratories, would have been a good place to start.

The furniture industry had already benefited from improved production machinery, but the power of information technology to improve responsiveness to market demand and time to market could only be dreamed of. Paper-based attempts at these tasks were a nightmare.

Other external impacts

- The severe winter of 1962–63 had boosted the demand for central heating in homes.

- England winning the World Cup in 1966 resulted in a mini-economic boom based on a 'feelgood' factor.

- Swinging London led the world in pop music and fashion in the mid-1960s.

The XYZ+20 team note in particular that 'Swinging London' did have an impact on the furniture industry. A niche market for new furniture concepts, 'something completely different', was established in the fashion streets of London. It became a nationwide market in the following decade.

The acid test

It is very interesting to look at history and consider how it affected our business and our industry. At the end of the exercise, we need to make a summary of what, out of everything we have looked at, should have been actionable, (with the benefit of hindsight) as in Table 5.2.

How was the market structured?

The team needs to move on to analyse the structure of the markets in which the company was operating. Who was adding what value, and where were they in the supply chain? Where was the power in the supply chain? Were there any external or abstract influencers? Who controlled information about the end consumers? How fierce was competition? Who were the competitors and what were their strengths and weaknesses compared to ours? Was it easy for others to enter the market, or for

TABLE 5.2 Summary of historical analysis

Topic	Item	Effect?
Politics and legislation	Attempts to suppress consumer demand	In hindsight, department store chains might have developed their own finance offerings in order to smooth out the effect of tax and credit controls.
	Safety	If anyone who took pride in the furniture industry could have foreseen the number of house fires in which fatalities were associated with quick burning foam in furniture, they might have seen some benefit in keeping ahead of legislative requirements. There might well have been an opportunity to provide a unique product to safety conscious consumers.
	Employment legislation	At the time, it seemed as if no political party was willing or able to take on the unions. The only way forward might have been to trade flexibility for higher pay or better conditions.
Economic cycles	Slump in 1972–74	Contingency plans have always been needed for boom and bust.
Social trends	Relative rise in prosperity – more consumers and new entrants to middle classes	There were opportunities galore to sell more furniture, but companies needed to second guess the buying behaviour of the next wave of entrants on the consumer scene. Perhaps if there had been some degree of joint market research in the industry, it would not have been so vulnerable to substitutes.
Technology changes	Manufacturing technology	The industry was pretty good at keeping up with the new technology, and needs to continue to do so.
	Information technology	Information technology was used as effectively as was believed feasible for the times. Perhaps more imagination could have been applied to using IT as a source of competitive advantage.

consumers to find substitutes? Was it possible for links in the value chain to be skipped or reconfigured?

In most industries the market map was simple and universal (Figure 5.2). Middlemen could survive by managing the risk of stockholding, as there was no IT available to support 'just-in-time' manufacturing.

Power was concentrated in the hands of the biggest department stores and chains, who placed their orders twice a year at furniture exhibitions. Relationships in the supply chain were probably adversarial, and were definitely based on one-off deals; there was no concept of partnership (Figure 5.3).

There were hidden forces at work in the market map. The industry association for furniture exerted some benign influence. As for gate-keepers, the people or organizations who might stop things happening in the market, it was the furniture workers' trade union, although the union activist on the XYZ+20 team insists that this was because management was as adversarial as his predecessors.

Where was the power in the market map?

The market map for the historical period, showing the forces of power in the market and based on Porter's Five Forces, is as illustrated in Figure 5.4.

FIGURE 5.2   Market map – generic

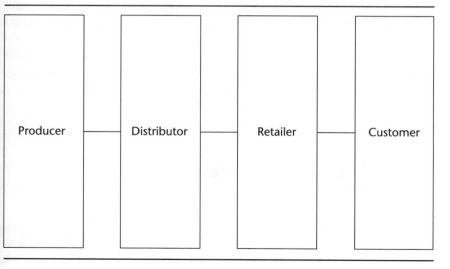

FIGURE 5.3   Market map – furniture in the 1960s

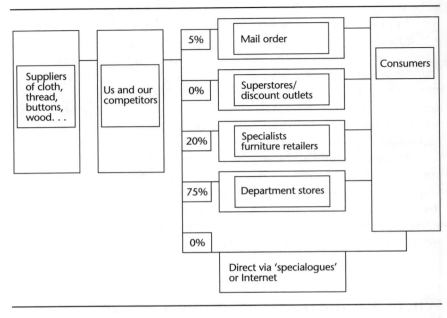

We can see from this model where the furniture manufacturers were most exposed about 25–30 years ago. Fashion furniture, made from alternative materials, was imported and retailed in new store concepts. Assembly panels from different materials for 'do-it-yourself' furniture were sold directly through warehouse style outlets. Alternatives succeeded because consumers were prepared to sacrifice quality for style and/or low prices, and because new competitors were able to offer new formulae in terms of materials and retail outlets (so they hit the whole supply chain at once). They were also able to circumvent the main gatekeeper (the trade union), and avoid the high capital costs of market entry.

Segmenting the value stages in the market map

Customers were not an amorphous mass, but individuals with differing lifestyles and tastes. This was recognized 20–30 years ago, but as there was not so much information around, ideas about 'segments' had to be

FIGURE 5.4   Forces of power in the furniture market – historical period

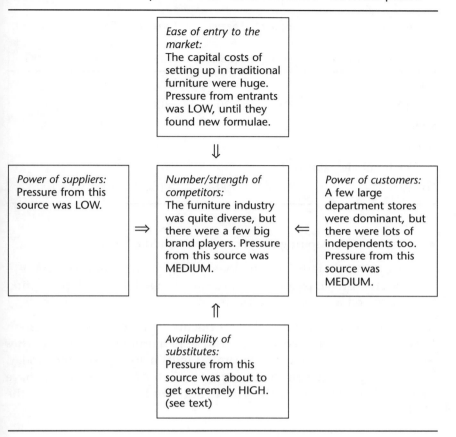

derived from indicators, such as occupation and newspaper readership (Table 5.3).

As in Chapter 4, we can define the market segments by their buying behaviour:

- *Segment A* – 'Classical' buyers: reasonably well-off, conservative people, probably in older age groups, most likely to buy from department stores offering personal service.

- *Segment B* – People on low incomes: always a significant segment.

- *Segment C* – People on lower middle incomes driven by practicalities, and the need for furniture to last a long time.

TABLE 5.3   Customer segmentation for the furniture market in the 1960s

Customers' buying criteria, 20–30 years ago	Segment A (30%)	Segment B (25%)	Segment C (15%)	Segment D (20%)	Segments E/F (10%)
Price	10	60	40	20	30
Quality	25	20	40	30	10
Style	25	20	0	20	40
Brand values	10	0	10	20	20
Service from sales staff	30	0	10	0	0
Totals	100%	100%	100%	100%	100%

- *Segment D* – Aspiring people on lower middle incomes.

- *Segment E* – fashion conscious young people and Segment F – lifestyle driven people, were probably merged in a small proportion of emerging 'hippy' consumers.

It seems quite plausible that these segments would have been universal. Needs do not change very much, just the proportions of different tastes for fulfilment. Our example company, as in its market positioning today, was focusing on Segment A. In the light of hindsight, XYZ might have thought about investing in the nascent Segment E/F, which had upset the market by 1972.

Why didn't they buy from us?

Table 5.4 analyses the weighting of buying criteria for Segment E/F and compares XYZ Ltd with a fashion concept store and a DIY furniture range

Although Segment E/F was price-driven in the 1970s, they were clearly the emergent middle class and thus would 'trade-up' in due course. In order to capture the new segment without sacrificing the old, the company could have adopted one or more of the following approaches:

- started importing as well as manufacturing, or copied imports;

- set up its own 'concept' stores and/or a concept catalogue;

- become a key supplier to the concept retailers.

TABLE 5.4 Buying criteria – XYZ and its competitors (Segment E/F)

Segment E/F Customers' buying criteria	Weight	Score, XYZ	Score × Weight	Score, fashion concept store	Score × Weight	Score, DIY	Score × Weight
Price	30	4	120	6	180	8	240
Quality	10	8	80	4	40	2	20
Style	40	3	120	9	360	0	0
Brand values	20	3	60	9	180	0	0
Totals			380		760		260

In fact, some of these options are still on the table for addressing XYZ's current position, and need to be discussed when the team establishes future scenarios.

The complete picture of the market is illustrated in Figure 5.5.

In the period being studied, 20–30 years ago, XYZ was well-positioned to serve Segments A and D. The company would have needed to invest more to meet the needs of Segment C, but it was of marginal interest or value to do so. XYZ could not match the DIY specialists in their pursuit of Segment B. History has not changed in that Segment E/F offered a dilemma – to invest or not to invest? If XYZ had been looking just a few years ahead, decision-makers would have considered it too high a risk, and indeed they did.

Now our review of history is complete. A summary is needed of the actionable elements of it. The XYZ+20 team conclude that, had they been able to see the 1990s from the past, they would have advocated that XYZ should have:

- known more about social trends and explored ways in which XYZ might have worked with the fashion furniture stores in order to gain some presence in the influential E/F Segment.

The question remains on the table for the XYZ+20 team, even if the company had chosen to overlook E/F, why had the company not been able to dominate in Segments A and D? In order to cover this territory, the XYZ+20 team conclude that, had they been able to see the 1990s from the past, they would have advocated that XYZ should have:

FIGURE 5.5   Attractiveness vs. performance matrix – historical period.
Note that the vertical axis runs from right to left. This may seem counter-intuitive, but it is the way the original designers intended it to be. Our focus is concentrated on the top left hand box. This box is based on the Directional Policy Matrix jointly developed by General Electric and McKinsey as illustrated in McDonald (1984).

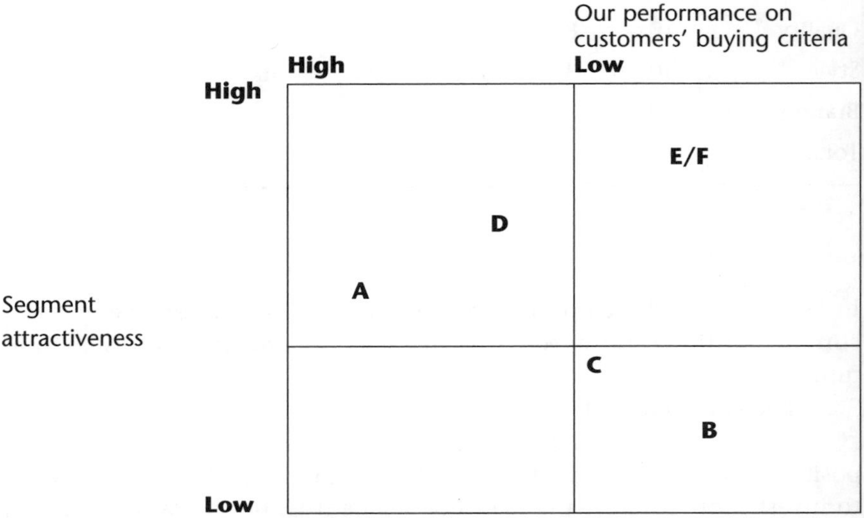

		Our performance on customers' buying criteria
	High	**Low**

High		E/F
	D	
A		
	C	
		B
Low		

Segment attractiveness

- been more pro-active on safety issues (in order to impress the 'practicals');

- sought more imaginative deals with the unions;

- explored the potential of information technology;

- tried to diffuse adversarial attitudes with department stores with high value, long-term arrangements, in order to gain more floor-space, which would provide more exposure of the XYZ products to the 'classicals'.

Having wallowed in the delights of hindsight, the team now braces itself for a leap into the future.

SUMMARY

In this chapter, we have established:

- what we were like as a going concern;

- what business we were in;

- what aspects of the business environment affected us;

- the structure of the market in the 1960s/1970s;

- where power lay in the market in the 1960s/1970s;

- what segments of the market were most attractive to us;

- the relative strengths and weaknesses we had in those segments;

- what hindsight tells us about how we might have bettered our position in the market.

Having seen how much our business changed in the past 20–30 years, in Chapter 6 we start to estimate how much it will change in the next 20–30 years.

CHAPTER SIX

Establishing the 'most likely' scenario

Sketching an aspirational view of the future

In this chapter, we shall carefully consider the future business environment and market structure. Anticipating customer needs and devising innovative ways to fulfil them deserves its own space and is therefore a separate step in the process, discussed in Chapter 7.

In considering the future, even before painting the background of the picture, the team has to decide how the company should be placed in that picture. Should it be dominant, or part of a group, a vignette in the corner or swooping down from the skies? It is helpful to start with a sketch, a hypothetical position for the business, rather than a blank sheet of paper. Such a sketch establishes a possibility for analysis.

The first thing the team can do is to establish what it thinks that the company ought to be achieving in 20–30 years' time. At this stage, vaunting ambition is to be encouraged, and the team may well assume that market leadership is the only proper aspirational starting point, however optimistic it may seem in the light of current circumstances.

Each member of the team should think, on their own initially, about what market leadership in 20–30 years time would look like in terms of key performance figures. Each view can then be presented to the team. (Questions may be taken, but no judgement should be expressed.) After all the presentations, the team can note similarities and where there are differences to be resolved. The view that seems most challenging ought to be adopted as the first sketch. There will be plenty of time later for applying liberal doses of caution to it. The purpose of building this long-term outlook is to seize a prosperous future.

If you do not raise your eyes, you will think you are the highest point.

Antonio Porchia

The XYZ+20 project team decides to start with a view of the future with XYZ as market leader, and proceeds to map what the company ought to look like as a going concern in 20–30 years time (Table 6.1).

- Will inflation have been eliminated?

- Will profitability have improved?

- Will stockholding be reduced even further?

- Will legal restrictions ensure debtor days are only 30?

- Will more or less people be employed?

For the XYZ+20 project team, the whole financial picture hinges on market share. They have to consider definitions of the market and what would constitute a dominant market share. They make the following assumptions in order to start their sketch:

- The size of the whole market for furniture will be similar to today in the UK and Europe.

TABLE 6.1   Key performance figures

	T + 20	*T + 21*	*T + 22*	*T + 23*	*Trend*
Sales volume					
Sales revenue					
Market share					
Gross margin					
Operating profit					
Capital employed					
Return on capital employed					
Stock turnover					
Debtor days					
Liquidity ratio					
People employed					

- The Department of Trade and Industry define a dominant market share as anything over 23 per cent, so 23 per cent ought to be XYZ's market share in the UK.

- XYZ will only have a prosperous future if it expands geographically. New outlets in Europe and partnerships with global retailers ought to mean XYZ doing twice as much overseas business as it does in the UK.

Working through all the calculations presents a picture to the team which seems miles away from the company's situation today, and an impossible dream. A graph is drawn to show the difference between this aspirational future position and an unqualified statistical trend based on the business carrying on as it is now (Figure 6.1).

The gap analysis graph is often referred to as the crocodile's jaws. The planning team may well feel like they are in the grip of a powerful and dangerous animal!

> The search for value has led companies to seek efficiency through downsizing, rationalising and right-sizing – approaches that eventually result in a diminishing level of return. But what will fuel growth in the future? Growth will come through mastering the skills of creativity – and making creativity actionable.
>
> *John Kao, Harvard Business School*

We see on the graph in Figure 6.1 an extreme case, that the pursuit of current strategies for the foreseeable future will result in a declining

FIGURE 6.1   Gap analysis

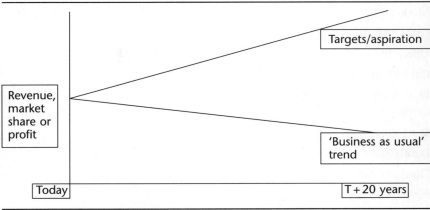

performance. If our company underinvests in capital equipment, marketing and skills, whilst concurrently increasing prices, customers will eventually lose interest, and someone else will come on to the market and make them a more attractive offer. Revenue will erode, and any short-term profits will indeed be temporary. (Downsizing has a lot in common with asset-stripping.)

Immediately we can see that our hypothetical 'business as usual' trend is flawed. The company would not last 20 years. We would imagine the company either going bankrupt or being taken over. This 'end of the line' scenario is a bullet rarely bitten in 5-year outlooks which show a pessimistic trend, but when we extend our horizon to 20 years it is clear that it could not go on indefinitely. The truth is that even if the company stands still rather than indulging in anorexia, the market 'herd' will stampede over it. Even reasonably positive 'business as usual' trends in the short term should show a tendency to decline (or collapse) in the long term, because it is impossible to maintain the status quo. The true gap that we have to map is between thriving and dying.

Now we have established an aspirational position and a 'business as usual' position, the time has come to use what we have learnt already and try to establish a 'most likely' scenario based on the factors of change in the market.

Establishing views of what the future will be like

Most of the management writers of the past few decades have extolled pure rationality in place of 'gut feelings' as intuition is often called. In fact, intuition cannot be divorced from rationality so easily. It is based on experience and learning, it is rarely a flight of complete fancy. Intuition and rationality are not opposing forces, but are complementary, which is why we can use factual analysis of the present and the past to fuel our intuition about the future. However, since we are naturally optimistic beings, we will have to test our 'rational' view with abstract thinking techniques, as discussed in Chapter 8.

There are many definitions of intuition, and none of them is completely right or wrong. All of the following can be incorporated in our understanding of the concept:

- *perception* – the identification of and extrapolation of patterns;

- *imagination* – through metaphor and representation (what is this situation like and how might it therefore develop);

- *visualization* – being able to describe a possible future.

The purpose of creating future views is to imagine the contexts in which customer needs might be fulfilled in the future, and what implication that has for products and services, and how they are delivered. We have noted how much change there has been in the world over the past 20 years. Now we have to consider how much change there will be in the next 20 years.

Building a future scenario is about raising our heads from the grindstone to imagine a really prosperous future. There is no point in trying to determine a future vision which is mediocre or depressing. At the same time, we have to develop our understanding of the future to determine what reality might really do to our business, and what we might really do about reality.

> The point of future scenarios . . . is not to trade exotic fictions . . . but to distinguish those features which are probably inevitable, and prepare ourselves for them, while identifying those elements which we could prevent if we were to act in time.
>
> *Charles Handy*

Scenario planning starts with a consideration of the purpose of the business and moves on to the impact of legislation, politics, economics, social trends and tastes, and technology. Each scenario must also incorporate a view of the business' specific industry – the market map (supply chain), including patterns of ownership, capital structure and financing. Attention also needs to be paid to competitors, and how they will behave.

What business will we be in?

Why will our organization exist? What customer needs will we be fulfilling and therefore what business will we be in? We need to establish what we will be helping our customers to achieve. Logically our mission ought to be the same as the one identified in the analysis of history and of today. Indeed, the XYZ+20 team have an easy task to imagine that XYZ will exist to provide comfort and aesthetics in people's homes. But some companies might not enjoy the luxury of a logical legacy with a logical future. However, that is no disadvantage to the team which is determined to seize the future.

Case study: Nokia

To take a sprawling, stumbling conglomerate and reshape it into a keenly focused, highly profitable company in the vanguard of one of the world's fastest growing industries is the stuff of management dreams.

Hugh Carnegy writing about Finnish telecommunications company Nokia in the Financial Times (10 July 1995)

Nokia was 130 years old when Jorma Ollila took over as Chief Executive in 1992. The company had lost a charismatic leader in the late 1980s and incurred heavy losses in the early 1990s. The company had been founded in 1865 as a forestry company, but by the 1960s had diversified. Once Ollila and his top team had decided that the future was telecommunications, other businesses (such as aluminium, tyres, power) were divested.

Case study: Virgin

Virgin demonstrates an opposite approach. Nokia seized their future by focus, Virgin seized its future by diversification. Having started out in the music business, the Virgin brand was extended to an airline, financial services, high technology accessories, rail transport and much more. Virgin's brand values mean a great deal to the company's enthusiastic customers, who believe that Virgin will gallop on a white charger into any industry where there is complacency and provide an excellent deal for the consumer. Most companies can only dream of having such a powerful market image.

Case study: The defence industry

The history of the defence industry has been a technological progression from weapons which could kill and injure an individual opponent to weapons of mass destruction. For many centuries, the premise driving the industry was that the greater the destruction that could be caused by a new machine of war, the greater the advantage gained by the government that bought it.

The future now required by the superpowers who are able to buy the best and the latest technology is quite different. Increasingly, these superpowers are deploying their armed forces in a peace-keeping role. Even for their war scenarios, it is being suggested that since war is an instrument of policy, killing people is not strictly necessary. The next lap of the arms race will feature non-lethal weapons (NLW).

What business environment/s will we operate in?

Every business will in 20–30 years' time, as ever, be affected by laws, economic cycles, social trends, technological change and other external impacts which cannot be controlled, such as the weather. How, given the likely forces in the business environment and changing market structures, how can we make sure our organization emerges as a winner? Dramatic change in business environments around the world can represent great opportunities or threats, and if we think far enough ahead we should be able to spot those which offer potential for our business.

The business environment interacts with the market structure, and will probably cause some kind of reconfiguration over a period of 20 years which we might not spot with a 5-year outlook. Technology in particular can take whole links out of the value chain, or lead to elements of quasi-integration such as information sharing which make the transfer of value look less like a chain and more like mixing the ingredients in a cake. Once again the team must consider the six key elements:

- What policies and legislation will affect us?

- How will the state of the economy affect our business?

- How will demographics affect us?

- What will social trends mean for our business?

- How much will technology do to us and for us?

- What other external impacts will have to be taken into account (e.g. weather)?

In considering the business environment, geographical scope is obviously relevant. Legislation and culture vary, therefore it is appropriate to choose one country at a time. A continental approach is acceptable if the team has the whole world to consider and if reasonable homogeneity can be assumed, e.g. North America, and increasingly, Europe.

The examples given here are not intended to be prescriptive. In the course of the past few years I have conducted many scenario planning sessions and in the next six sub-sections the descriptions in italic print are illustrative of the usual consensus items in teams' lists. The probable conclusions of our fictional XYZ+20 team are put forward in boxed text. In Chapter 8, we will test their cosily rational outlook.

Policies and legislation

In building future scenarios, it is important to think about the mundane and universal controls which might affect the business environment as well as the specifics. If we can be better prepared for legislation, it will give us a cost advantage over competition.

What sorts of laws will we have to live with?
Examples to protect shareholders and/or stockholders are:

- fiduciary duties of directors and directors' duty of care;

- company law.

There has been a steady trend of increasing protection for shareholders. As more 'ordinary' people get involved in shareholding, it seems reasonable to expect more of the same.

> The XYZ+20 expect the company to be offering share ownership schemes which will bind employees and supply chain partners closer to the company.

Legislation to protect employees may be in the areas of:

- health and safety;

- equal opportunities;

- employment law, governing individuals' rights at work (e.g. against unfair dismissal).

There are conflicting trends here.

In the USA, the UK and Asia, collective rights embodied in trade unions hardly exist (although in the UK they were once strong); in most European countries trade unions do still have some rights. The UK situation of the late 1970s, in which prolonged, extremely disruptive and emotive labour unrest persuaded voters to elect a government pledged to constrain those rights, could be repeated in any of the countries of mainland Europe in the next 20 years, and might affect the whole European Union.

Control of the working environment may still seem a good cause in developed and developing economies, and many global companies are determined to be in the lead (e.g. BP, who have a rigorous approach to health and safety).

Many companies are still struggling to avoid exposure to claims from individual rights at work legislation. One response has been to reduce the number of employees in favour of contractors or 'temps'. To a legislator, this is a loophole ripe for closure. The rights of employees might well be extended to contractors and 'out-sourced' staff. Indeed, in the European Union, the 'transfer of undertakings' legislation is a step on the way to this.

However, some rights might become conditional, especially to protect small businesses. For example, the requirement for a job to be held open throughout a long illness might be made conditional on an insurance policy which protects both the employee and the employer from loss of income as a result.

Meanwhile, there could be wider legislative changes which affect the nature of the workforce, e.g. raising the retirement age to reduce public spending on pensions which would be likely to be accompanied by the banning of age discrimination in the workplace.

The complexities are such that a positive approach to the spirit of employment law, which is to improve the quality of life of people at work, is the prudent strategy.

The XYZ+20 team decide that it would be in the company's interest, with the trade union as a partner, to help employees with the heavy pension and insurance burden they will face. In return the company is bound to expect additional flexibility in working arrangements.

Legislative measures to protect customers encompass:

- consumer protection
- supply chain controls
- professional liability insurance

Once again we see a steady trend of increased protection for the consumer – indeed sellers might protest that consumers are even protected from their own omission and/or neglect. The team might have difficulty imagining consumer law getting any tighter, but there will be areas of activity. For example, it is considered by many consumer lobby interests that the information that selling companies hold about individual consumers is not treated with sufficient care and confidentiality. Telemarketing companies and credit control agencies are particularly likely targets for more control.

Health scares may also force the issue of the traceability of products into law. For example, the BSE crisis ('mad cow' disease) has led farmers and food producers to expect that within a short period of time, food items will have to be traceable from the supermarket shelf to the original breeder or grower (and the parent animal).

In the USA, a 50-year-old law holds company buying professionals liable for their suppliers' illegal labour practices, even if they take place outside the USA. Concern in European markets about issues such as child labour in developing countries may hasten similar legislation.

The XYZ+20 team are struck with the impression that information is power, and consumers are already demanding it. Partnerships and open information exchange throughout the supply chain will be essential. In addition, working with safety organizations, and reassuring customers that XYZ is implementing the latest safety ideas, could deliver competitive advantage.

To protect the community in which we operate there may be legislation in the areas of:

- tax and duties;

- planning regulations (use of land, premises, etc.);

- public liability insurance;

- environmental regulations.

The writing is already on the wall in Europe – the environmental laws of 2020 are expected to be draconian in comparison to the weedy and ill-enforced pollution laws of today! Partial car bans are already used regularly in Athens and occasionally in Paris. Car drivers may find themselves as ostracized as smokers! Progress towards greater environmental control is likely to be slower in other parts of the world, but the trend is still the same.

Once again, the benefits of getting ahead of the legislative bulldozer are evident. Initiatives such as the use of video-conferencing to minimize travel, a distribution fleet run on gas rather than diesel, and examining the potential use of solar energy in the factory should be investigated. XYZ is already supporting charities who redistribute second-hand furniture to people in need, and the company could be more directly involved in the collection and distribution of second-hand furniture.

Legislation to protect suppliers is concerned with the areas of:

- copyright;

- contract law.

Partnership sourcing is encouraged at the moment, and many of the trends on issues such as traceability and ethics suggest that it will be more commonplace in years to come. This may mean that contract law becomes more complex in order to cover 'in perpetuity' contracts as well as 'one-off' transactions.

As previously mentioned, the XYZ+20 team are convinced of the need for closer relationships and information-sharing throughout the supply chain.

I can guarantee that if all these issues had been discussed in a company planning for a 3–5 year outlook, the team's conclusion would be that 'nothing much will change within the timeframe of this plan'. When we think about a 20 year outlook, it is easier to see that the legislative environment for business is unlikely to get any easier and plans are required for punitive environmental legislation in Europe just as surely as they are needed for a single European currency.

We also have to prepare for the possibility of laws specifically affecting our industry. Examples of possible industry-specific laws are:

- Financial services
  This industry is likely to become more regulated due to the perceived failure of self-regulation.

- Construction, agriculture, etc.
  Land use laws are also likely to become more intrusive, due to environmental concerns.

- Pharmaceutical, food and drink
  The trend of campaigns on health issues to do with food and drugs is that most substances and processes should be controlled, including:
  – all addictive drugs including nicotine and alcohol,
  – genetically altered food,
  – prescription drugs,
  – alternative remedies,
  – cosmiceuticals (cosmetics combined with pharmaceutical treatments),
  – nutriceuticals (food with health additives, etc.),
  – research processes such as testing on animals,
  – clinical tests.

However, a backlash from the perceived over-protection of consumers in 'the beef crisis' might be demands on governments just to inform people about risks (as they do with cigarettes) and leave them to make their choices.

As was said earlier, new laws are a fact of life. As the complexity of life increases, voters demand more complex laws. If we study the policies of relevant political parties and interest groups with widespread popular support, we know they will cause change. The knack is to spot the minority organizations whose popular support is accelerating. For example, in the UK, campaigns against the transport of live animals and campaigns against road building have attracted middle-aged, middle class ladies to the barricades alongside young enthusiasts. More recently, the campaign to legalize cannabis, especially for medical purposes, has gained respectability.

> The XYZ+20 team perceive that the main challenge to the furniture industry will be to ensure the highest safety standards and to provide information about the sources of fabrics, wood and other components, and manufacturing processes.

Economic cycles

When I was chancellor I was bombarded with neat econometric models and tidy economic projections. Some of them helped you to think or gave you something useful to argue about, but, in general, most of them had absolutely no bearing on what was actually going on. . . . If it comes to a choice between anecdotal evidence and the latest economic model I would always go for the anecdotes.
                    Kenneth Clarke, former UK Chancellor of the Exchequer

Well, the word on the street is that mature economies can only ever hope for modest growth (say an average of 2 per cent per annum), but history suggests that economies always find new pockets of growth from somewhere. Can this really be sustainable if the population is declining, and if environmental fundamentalism forces an anti-growth political environment? Prudence is to plan for the average and have contingency plans for booms and busts.

In developing economies, the prudent plan is for high growth, which needs to be accompanied by a contingency plan for occasional severe setbacks (as occurred in Indonesia, South Korea and Malaysia in 1997).

The XYZ+20 team are excited about the prospect of developing a detailed contingency plan for recovery from a recession. They believe that it would be an opportunity to gain a sizeable chunk of market share.

Demographics

In 20 years time, baby boomers will be in their 60s and 70s. This is the generation which, when it had time on its hands as students, was particularly rebellious. As retirees, they may be rebellious again. They may display a high degree of individuality as consumers.

The opinion leaders will be the teenagers of today – so what are their views and how likely are they to take them into middle age? Most parents note that their children seem to want to be 'casual' in style, but they are also very brand conscious, often due to peer pressure. They are at ease with technology, and tolerant of a wider variety of lifestyles than parents tend to be. As adult consumers, they might show devout brand loyalty, but demand price decreases; and they might prefer to shop from computer screens.

The XYZ+20 team can see great advantages in being the first choice of the older generation in 2020, but of course, it would not be enough to sustain the company until 2050! Sub-branding of different styles and designs might be a route to dominance in several market segments.

Social trends

It is expected that the 'green' movement will continue to go from strength to strength. Some people see it as an ideological trend which could get as big as communism was in the early part of the twentieth century, some even see equally dire consequences, such as eco-terrorism.

However, it is more likely that fear of crime will create elements of totalitarianism in society, with cameras and alarms everywhere. Civil liberties lobbyists will lose their arguments as citizens demand defence of their persons and property.

Politicians will be as anxious as ever to promote family values, but the concept of family will have changed in many societies. People may see advantages in living with others rather than living alone, but the nuclear family will not be the only configuration. Even so, UK government housing projections for 2006 assume a great deal more people in all age groups will be living alone.

Health lobbyists have scared many prosperous individuals into protecting themselves via healthy lifestyles, whilst the overall physical health of the nation declines due to over-eating and under-exercising. Meanwhile, the cases of mental illness of varying degrees of severity rises and rises. There may be a backlash against stress, especially work-induced stress. It has been the topic of several high profile court cases in which defendants have won considerable damages against employers who were deemed to have piled stress upon them.

XYZ will need to produce furniture specifically for small households, will have to demonstrate its environmental credentials, and will also have to incorporate health considerations into products, such as ergonomics and aromatherapy.

Technology

The unstaunchable march of technology may be arrested by the Millennium bug, and theoretically, there could be a limit to how much data capacity you can squeeze on to a silicon chip. Nevertheless, the reasonable scenario for 2020+ is that technology will still be with us and to a greater degree than today. Mobile phones, video recorders and microwave ovens were unheard of 25 years ago, outside of science fiction. (Arthur C Clarke, writing in the 1960s, predicted many of the electronic gizmos that we hold dear today.)

We might consider what electronic gizmos will dominate our lives in 2020+. Video phones are likely to be commonplace (hologram phones are forecast for 2016), together with combined television/computers offering interactive entertainment, shopping, home management and work.

Telecommuting will be commonplace, to beat the car bans. Virtual reality exercise machines will be required to counteract sedentary lifestyles.

Technology will also be more dominant in the world of work in our 'most likely' scenario. It has been claimed that electronic data interchange alone can reduce transaction costs between companies by 90 per cent. Companies with global reach already rely internally and externally on e-mail communications. In some cases, business contacts have to build up relationships via e-mail. Businesses will use flexible information systems to progress to process integration, with other organizations and even with end customers.

At the graphical user interface, things will get easier and easier. This will reduce the mystique of computer skills, enough to enable technophobes and the older generation to gain advantage from 'high tech' facilities.

If XYZ is market leader, it will be using technology as much as possible to make its processes better, cheaper and faster, and it will be using components like smart fabrics which can warm up or cool down according to the room temperature. Technology also offers the opportunity for new product lines associated with the office within the home. It is also feasible that the Internet will be well-enough developed to enable the selling of furniture directly to consumers, alongside or within traditional retail outlets.

Other external impacts

Weather models have been reasonably successful in predicting average weather patterns over long periods of time. It is generally expected that in the next 20–30 years, average world temperatures will rise by about 1°C. However, it is the increasing volatility of the weather also seems to be a trend we are going to have to live with, and which the models cannot track so well. Even if we do reduce emissions of greenhouse gases, those industries which are affected by the weather need to plan for extreme scenarios. For example, the east of England has had periods in the past few years with less rain than Jerusalem, hence the local water company plans to build desalination plants off the coast.

XYZ will be producing more portable, adjustable, versatile and durable furniture for all seasons.

The acid test

After exploring all possibilities, the project team needs to make a summary of what, out of everything they have looked at, is actionable. After all, we need to use our glimpses of the far future to ensure that our 3–5 year plan is vigorous enough to ensure we seize the future before anybody else does. Table 6.2 draws together the possibilities and the team starts to see some exciting ways forward which can be incorporated in shorter term plans.

How is the market structured?

The team also needs to analyse the structure of the markets in which the company will operate. Who will add what value, and where will they be placed in the supply chain? Where will power lie in the supply chain? Will there be any external or abstract influencers? Who will control information about the end consumers? How fierce will competition be? What links in the value chain will have been skipped or reconfigured? A possible generic market structure for 2020 is shown in Figure 6.2, while a market map for furniture is illustrated in Figure 6.3.

Within 20 years we might believe that retailers will have a much harder job justifying the value they bring to a buying proposition. In the USA, visits to malls are already decreasing so dramatically that retailers are transforming themselves into entertainment experiences in order to compete with TV and electronic shopping.

If we follow through all the trends in the business environment, the market structure for furniture in the UK ought to look something like the illustration in Figure 6.3. As a large, bulky item of household comfort, a mix of outlets will probably still be needed. There will be more choice in terms of a route to market, for the producer and the consumer, with the growth being in direct communications between producer and consumer via electronic methods.

The percentages shown in Figure 6.3 might be regarded as exaggerated today, but exaggeration is important to improve our understanding of the potential for changes in the power structure in the supply chain and for imagining new routes to market. It is quite feasible that by 2020, manufacturers could re-establish their own branding and gain leverage which retailers will have to respect.

TABLE 6.2 Summary analysis for the future

Topic	Item	Gap?
Politics/ legislation	Safety regulations. e.g. fire resistant materials	▪ Work with safety organizations ▪ Reassuring customers that XYZ is implementing the latest safety ideas
	Environmental legislation	▪ Initiatives such as the use of video-conferencing to minimize travel, a distribution fleet run on gas rather than diesel, and examining the potential use of solar energy in the factory should be investigated ▪ Be more directly involved in the collection and distribution of second hand furniture to the needy
Economic cycles	Assume modest growth	▪ Developing a detailed contingency plan for recovery from a recession
Demographics		▪ Be the first choice of the older generation ▪ Use sub-branding to develop new styles and designs to address other market segments
Social trends	Health issues, family variation	▪ Produce furniture specifically for small households ▪ Demonstrate environmental credentials ▪ Incorporate health considerations into products, such as ergonomics and aromatherapy
Technology changes		▪ Use technology to make processes better, cheaper and faster ▪ Research components like smart fabrics which can warm up or cool down according to the room temperature ▪ Address the needs of consumers with an office within their home ▪ Sell furniture over the Internet
Other	Warmer weather	▪ Produce more portable, adjustable, versatile and durable furniture for all seasons

FIGURE 6.2   Market map for 2020 – generic

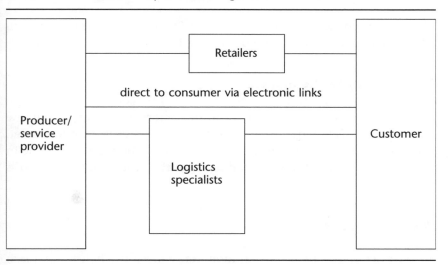

FIGURE 6.3   Market map for 2020 – XYZ Furniture

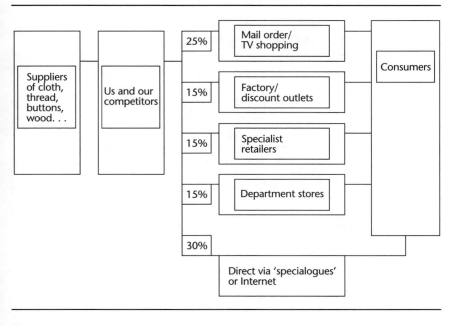

Where is the power in the market map?

The team needs to consider each of the five forces and how they will affect the market in which the business will be operating (Figure 6.4).

Ease of entry to the market

It is not impossible to start a furniture factory in a garage, but the economies of scale required to be a major player, even in one market, would be a deterrent to most potential entrants. The future might lie in mail order furniture from developing countries where craftsmanship is still relatively cheap.

Power of suppliers

We have perceived a probable transition from a linear to a holistic approach to the value chain, shown in graphical form in Figure 6.5. Companies are being driven towards closer relationships with strategic suppliers by the need for traceability and lean supply (e.g. just-in-time delivery). This trend diffuses the power struggle between suppliers and customers. It is also

FIGURE 6.4   Forces of power in the furniture market – the future

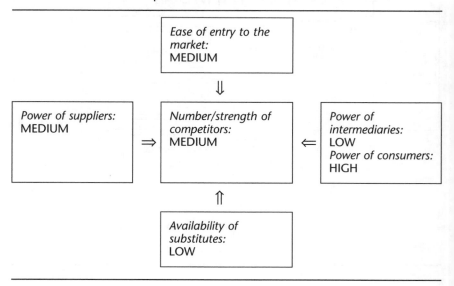

FIGURE 6.5 The changing nature of supply chains. From MacDonald and Rogers (1998)

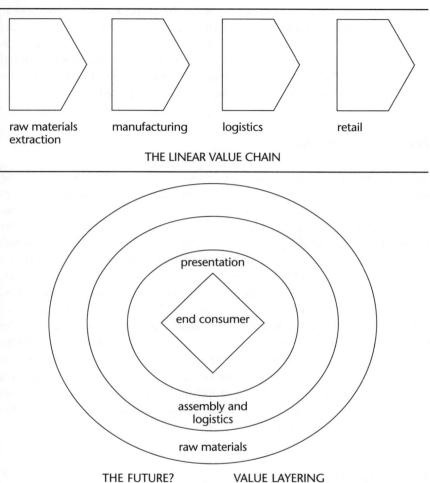

raw materials extraction   manufacturing   logistics   retail

THE LINEAR VALUE CHAIN

presentation

end consumer

assembly and logistics

raw materials

THE FUTURE?   VALUE LAYERING

unlikely in this market that suppliers of furniture raw materials would want to leapfrog manufacturers to make any direct offers to retailers or consumers.

Number and strength of competitors

There will continue to be many, diverse competitors. Due to the dominance of taste and lifestyle in the industry, there will be plenty of choice for producers and consumers. Retailers may wish to defend their role in the value chain via own-branding, which could threaten manufacturers' brands. It is also likely that competition will assume wider geographical scope. Since furniture is bulky and has some cultural attributes, it is not likely to become a global industry, although some manufacturers may be lucky enough to forge partnerships with global retailers. Nevertheless, it would be easy to supply most of Europe from the UK, and electronic shopping could ease entry to those markets.

Power of customers

Retailers will be on the defensive, and it is likely that there will be consolidation of department store and furniture chains. Retailing has always promoted itself as a leisure activity, but much more evidence of entertainment elements will be required in order to motivate people to shop. The potential for partnership with retailers may be attractive, but only a few pursuing global strategies will be able to offer opportunities for expansion.

The consumer will have more choice of outlets and more power, which will probably bring the price of even the most differentiated product under pressure. The customer may have always been hailed as king, but was not always a very well-informed monarch. In 2020, the consumer will choose to be very well informed. The concept of adding value is significant. Consumers need raw materials to be converted into something they can use, transported to where they need them and presented to them for selection. Shopping in retail outlets may be time-consuming and full of 'hassle factors'. Shopping from home may also have disadvantages, but it will be a preferred option for some consumers.

Availability of substitutes

Could it be that novelty 'no wood, no foam' furniture will be promoted by the green movement to save trees? This is one possibility, but the main substitute feared for the far future is a denial of consumption. Environmental fundamentalism may lead to a category of new consumer who consumes less than previous generations.

We can see from this model where the XYZ Furniture company can go in the next 20–30 years. It could expand out of the UK into culturally similar European markets. It could serve 'multiple niches' with heavily branded, lifestyle offerings. It could establish direct links with consumers, perhaps via direct mail initially, but ultimately by electronic methods, whilst choosing strategic suppliers, a delivery company and a few select retailers as potential partners.

Next, the team should discuss how the apparent opportunities to expand affect the framework of ownership, capital investment and financial resources of the company. Will the industry and this business in particular become more concentrated in the ownership of a few people, or will it fragment? Will it be high tech or low tech? What will its capital gearing be like? What are the cash flow implications of the scenario? For example, direct sales to customers may improve cash flow and create easier opportunities for organic growth.

For the XYZ+20 team, the framework of ownership is a sensitive topic. The project team sponsor is a member of the family which has owned the company for a century. Nevertheless, the team are required to cover all aspects of possible 2020 scenarios. They consider that it would be possible to finance growth from profits only if growth were very gradual. Acquisitions, which might be expedient in terms of gaining market share, would have to be financed by borrowing. They also assume that a wider share ownership will be inevitable in the future, as share incentives will be needed to cement partnerships with employees and other stakeholders.

Blocking competitors

One of the critical sources of advantage will be in strategically blocking the progress of competitors. They are not going to stand still whilst our XYZ Furniture company fulfils its strategy. Classically, blocking competitors meant seizing market share and setting up barriers to entry, but since the market map is subject to much greater flux in recent times than ever before, a number of mistakes have been made, and these will now be briefly considered.

Ignoring some competitors

Just because competitors are not an immediate threat does not mean they could not change, or even take over: discounters can go up-market; niche players can broaden their appeal. However, these things do not happen overnight. Awareness of competitor activity is crucial so that early hints of activity can be monitored and a response worked out.

Allowing existing competitive advantage to fade

Even market leaders are often caught out by competitors' moves on to their territory. They may have become complacent and left room for a competitor to come along with a better offer. In this case, the furniture company needs to maintain steady investment in its traditional strengths in the classics before investing aggressively in other market segments.

Launching new initiatives in a tactical rather than strategic way, without assessing competitive responses

Many companies who start price wars live to regret it. Offering a new service which can be easily copied delivers only a temporary tactical advantage. In the UK when one bank decided to extend its opening hours, it was a great success with customers and did attract some new business in the short-term, until all the other banks did the same.

Market leaders will adopt strategies which are not so easy to copy, and provide more intangible advantages in the market place, such as:

- product innovation;

- process innovation;

- a strong reputation for something ethical, such as concern for consumer safety or environmental activities;

- partnerships with strategic suppliers to achieve synergy in the market;

- customer loyalty through relationship-building;

- outstanding design.

Failure to understand competitors' likely reactions

If the XYZ Furniture company makes a strategic move, something dramatic which changes the rules of the market, responses will vary:

- some competitors will ignore it (this could be a surprisingly large proportion);

- some will respond selectively;

- some will retaliate in panic;

- some will try to change the rules back or on to a new platform.

From what we have seen of our competitors in the past, we ought to be able to categorize them and monitor them accordingly. Building a good scenario for the very long term does not absolve a business from the responsibility to adopt nimble tactics as the future begins to unfold. Competitive reactions have to be extremely carefully handled. A summary of likely competitor reactions is shown in Table 6.3.

The project team must think as their counterparts in the competitors would think – many failures of military strategy have been due to a failure to see things from the enemy's point of view. The plotting of the competitor responses should emphasize the need to implement creative alternatives – changing the rules of engagement. It also demonstrates the need to aim for long-term success rather than short-term gains or immediate avoidance of loss. The team needs to develop those creative alternatives to gain advantage and block competitors with a strong brand, or cost, scope, process or relationship advantages.

The XYZ+20 team establish that their first priority is to be in charge of changing the rules of the game. They also conclude that if XYZ is market leader in 2020, it will not have been through taking part in a price war or short-term gimmicks.

SUMMARY

In this chapter, we have established:

- what we will be like as a going concern;

- what business we will be in;

- what aspects of the business environment will affect us;

- the likely future structure of the market;

- where power will lie in the market;

- how we need to counteract the activity of competitors.

In Chapter 7, we move on to discuss how the needs of customers must drive our long-term view.

TABLE 6.3   Plotting the reactions of the competition

	XYZ	*WQR*	*ASY*	*'Green' substitute*
Category of competition		Selective response	Ignore it	Change the rules
Business strategy	Multi-niche	Try different niches	Generalists	Dominate one niche completely
Marketing	'Specialogue mail order	Will copy	Continue to sell to retailers	Network marketing to save paper
Manufacturing	Hi-tech plus crafting	Will not invest	Hi-tech	As little as possible
Development	Innovative, highly branded designs	Will bring out look-alikes	Classic, low-risk styles	Style subservient to content
Finance	Diversify ownership and capital, aim for better cash flow and organic growth	Highly geared	Family dominant	Backed by charities
Human resources	Highly skilled, motivated staff	Highly skilled, motivated staff	Adversarial	Staff ideologically committed

Adapted from Kotler (1991).

CHAPTER SEVEN

Identifying future customer needs

What customer needs are fulfilled?

I'll tell you what I want, what I really, really want!

The Spice Girls

Even the sceptical creator of Dilbert says that companies will be prosperous if they are providing products or services that customers really want. If only customers would tell their suppliers what they really, really want! Guidance from customers can be very helpful in identifying incremental improvements in products, processes and services, but when it comes to seizing the future, the burden is on suppliers to invent, to imagine the next generation of products and services to fulfil certain observable customer needs. That, of course, is high risk. But we can minimize that risk. We can minimize it first of all by looking at it in the context of our future scenario. We have already considered what trends are most likely to be driving customer needs and tastes.

We have studied the potential future structure of the market in which we expect to be operating. We also have to ask why the market should exist at all. What needs will be fulfilled? How might they be fulfilled? Future customer needs must be explored in great detail as a topic in its own right, because fulfilling them more successfully and sooner than competitors should lead to the prosperous future we have imagined.

Inventing a product and then looking for a need to fulfil has had its outstanding successes – such as the Post-it note – and nine times as many failures. The team ought to have plenty of time for some free-form brainstorming to generate large quantities of ideas for future products, processes and services. At a conceptual level, it is perfectly permissible to explore the technically possible, provided developers understand that it eventually has to be linked to need, and if this is not possible then it must be shelved.

Of course, we could also approach it from the other direction. Most successful entrepreneurs have identified a need, studied it, and set out to meet it in a very systematic way.

In fact, there are two fundamental critical success factors for the products and services our business might produce in the future:

- they must fulfil some category of need;

- in the fulfilment of that need, they must either take hassle out of, or add enjoyment to people's lives.

Reducing 'hassle' cannot be stressed enough. Many people will pay handsomely for any product or service which saves them time or bother.

A useful conceptual model to help us to understand the challenges involved in fulfilling future needs is shown in Figure 7.1.

The different types of need described – specific, vague, bespoke and evolving – are present in most business to business markets, although sometimes in very different proportions. Evolving needs are rarely encountered in consumer markets. Depending on what type of need you are setting out to fulfil with your product, the risks vary and therefore also the probability of success. If you know that the need you are setting out to fulfil is simple and well-established, and all you have to do is provide a product which fulfils it better, cheaper and faster, the risks are

FIGURE 7.1 A need fulfilment matrix. From Rogers (1996)

	Type of use: Straightforward	Difficult to define or multi-faceted concept
Number of users:		
Many	SPECIFIC	VAGUE
Few	BESPOKE	EVOLVING
	Lower risk	Higher risk

low, but the rewards may be low as well. Less well-defined needs demand high levels of creativity in the solution, but will deliver higher benefits over time, albeit sometimes a long period of time. When introduced to the telephone, one far-sighted businessman exclaimed: 'It's a wonderful invention! I can see the day when every town in America will have one!' It was one of those inventions where the inventor's descendants were likely to gain more benefit that he ever could.

Specific needs

Specific needs require a finite, commodity product to fulfil them. A successful solution usually exists, therefore the product/service development challenge is product enhancement – a better, cheaper, or faster solution.

Specific needs can be described very simply, they are well under-stood, and apply to a great number of people. Glue is a household staple because so many people have a need to stick things together, and people buy drills because they have a need to make holes. The following five cases demonstrate how existing products concepts can be improved enough to establish a new generation product or service approach.

Case 1: Removing dust from carpets

The concept of a vacuum cleaner was invented in 1901 by a British engineer, and a domestic model was developed in 1908 by an American janitor, who sold the patent to W H Hoover. From then until the 1980s, Hoover was the dominant brand in the UK, and had even been absorbed into the dictionary. British people talked about 'doing the hoovering', 'I hoovered the bedroom', etc.

In the 1980s, British inventor James Dyson developed a much improved design for a vacuum cleaner. He offered to sell the design to European brand leaders, but they snubbed him. So, via business ventures in the USA and Japan, Dyson raised enough capital to start up on his own. By 1997, Dyson had achieved a dominant market share with his formula – a see-through vacuum cleaner without a bag, and with special dust filters. The British were hoovering with their Dysons. James Dyson had not invented the concept of the vacuum cleaner, but he had worked out a better way to fulfil the specific need people have to remove dust from their carpets.

Electrolux have now made a quantum leap in home cleaning by inventing an ingenious robot vacuum cleaner, which moves around the house using in-built radar, cleaning without human intervention. Hard-pressed housewives who tested the prototype raved about its quiet efficiency and 'gentleness'! By 2020, homes are expected to be full of robotic labour-saving devices.

Case 2: Making holes in things

Drills are drills. People need them to make holes in things. The first electric drill was a great, labour-saving breakthrough. However, the leads were a bit of a hazard. When Black and Decker first introduced extra long leads, it was a minor change which proved enormously popular with customers. The advent of the cordless drill was even more welcome. The specific need for making holes was being fulfilled in a much more convenient and safe way.

Case 3: Receiving health information

British inventor Trevor Baylis was concerned when he heard that health education in Africa was being hampered because people could not afford batteries to power the radios which could deliver the health education messages, (as well as much more information and entertainment). He developed a clockwork radio. Despite intensive media interest, it was some time before a backer was found to ensure that the product was produced commercially in South Africa. It is now available in European markets as well. Once again, we see in this case that an existing product which fulfilled an existing need was reworked in a truly innovative way to open up new markets and provide more choice in existing ones.

Case 4: Comfort and utility when away from home

In the 1980s, a hotel chain in the US paused before upgrading bedroom televisions. An analysis of calls to housekeeping revealed that two thirds of them were to request an iron and ironing board. So the hotel chain used the budget for TV upgrades to put irons and ironing boards in all rooms instead. It fulfilled a specific service need that customers were expressing to them, and it improved the productivity of the housekeeping department.

Case 5: Just two of the many examples from the innovative culture of 3M

Trizact is a new polishing material. 3M's original business was manufacturing sandpaper, and it has now utilized a technology previously applied in other products, such as reflective road signs, to create an abrasive belt which delivers significant time and cost savings to the customer.

3M's ScotchBrite Never Rust Soap Pads, made from recycled plastic bottles, captured over 20 per cent of the American market for scouring pads from rusting, splintering steel wool within 18 months of their launch.

The search for more and better solutions to specific needs is always on. Microchip technology has been applied to household appliances to achieve better quality, and chemicals are mixed and remixed in pursuit of the best washing powder.

If we are fulfilling a well-known, well-expressed, well-understood and widespread need, we can reasonably assume that need will be around in 20 years' time. Our furniture company can feel confident that comfort and storage in the home will be needed as much in 2030 as it was in 1930. The challenge is, customers will be demanding new functionality and aesthetics, and expecting more choice.

We should not assume that all specific needs already have an obvious product or service to fit. It is possible to come across specific needs which are not properly addressed, usually in emerging market segments. For example, most of the developed world expects large increases in the number of elderly consumers during the next 30 years, and with it 'grey power'. Older people have a number of specific needs which are overlooked by consumer goods suppliers in pursuit of the 'average' consumer or the high-spending younger consumer. A successful boat builder designed a tipping orthopaedic bath for the elderly in 1978 and ran away with a £21 million market.

The XYZ+20 team are convinced that they can see immediate potential for better fulfilment of specific customer needs, such as more durable, washable, stain-resistant, comfortable covers for chairs, better closing mechanisms on cupboards, scratch resistant table tops, adjustable chairs, heated chairs, and lifting seats in chairs to help the elderly.

Bespoke needs

There are needs which are quite straightforward, but because they are required by only a few individuals or organizations, the solution can be tailored for each customer or group of customers. The addition or exclusion of features for each customization also serves to develop the product concept as a whole. The ideal example of bespoke needs is computer services.

A set of generic tools and skills, tailored to each customer's requirements, also characterizes cleaning services, catering, building and decorating. Many business to business products and services fulfil bespoke needs, but bespoke needs also exert influence in some consumer industries, such as fashion.

Case 6: The business need for reliable, speedy information systems

In the early days of computing, software was written for each computer system and each customer's particular application. Each customer wanted a system fashioned to their particular needs. In time, programmers worked out how core, reusable code could be developed. This trend was accelerated by the arrival in the late 1970s of mini-computers with easier programming languages. Companies buying mini-computers usually engaged software houses to install their core software packages and customize them. When personal computers were launched, software packages became finite 'shrink-wrapped' products (what you see is what you get). As needs and the market to serve them progressed, the transition was made from bespoke to specific. More businesses wanted software, so software became commoditized.

Case 7: The business need for a clean working environment

ISS provide cleaning services, something that is often regarded as the most commoditized of all services. But to some companies, cleaning has a strategic role, and they require highly differentiated services from their contractors. This is true of food companies, and companies to whom cleanliness is part of their image. ISS pay high wages to their staff and train them to be very good cleaners, able to meet demanding output expectations. They will also take on other tasks for clients. For example, where they have contracts for cleaning public buildings, staff may be trained in the layout of the buildings and how to give directions to visiting members of the public.

There are movements between the specific and bespoke box, and cross-fertilization can be a source of innovation. Which of the needs described as bespoke now, will gain mass market appeal in the future thus demanding that products/services to fulfil them will become standardized and commoditized in the future? Cars were individualized until Henry Ford's production line. Now, car manufacturers are using information systems links with dealers to offer more options to customers, so the trend is reversing to some degree.

Which products or services that now are standardized and commoditized can be made more personal in the future? Almost any 'slow-moving' consumer product, and certainly high value goods in business to business markets can be tailored more closely to the tastes of the few, or even the individual, as a result of the speed and complexity of information that can be exchanged between buyer and seller. In the case of our furniture manufacturer, the future is very likely to involve more flexibility and build to order.

The XYZ+20 team can see potential for the company to provide special services to hotels, such as providing bespoke 'themed furniture' (maritime theme, nostalgic theme, environmental theme) which might have knock-on benefits in consumer markets.

Vague needs

Having reviewed the 'low risk' side of the matrix, we now need to move on to the 'high risk' side of needs fulfilment. The difference between specific needs and vague needs is often defined as needs which are already satisfied (specific) and needs which as yet are unsatisfied (vague). Very often, the customer does not know that they have an unsatisfied need until presented with the solution. There are often layers of vague, unexpressed and unsatisfied needs wrapped around known generic needs. So there is plenty of scope for innovation. Microsoft have turned a group of their software developers into detectives, studying the habits of office workers in order to find software solutions to support them.

Fulfilment of vague needs is what wins a company a reputation for innovation. It requires a high degree of deliberate creativity, and can result in very high rewards. Vague needs are not easy to describe and very difficult to research. They are the needs which we hint at in our behaviour, but do not express. Who knew they needed Post-it notes before Post-it notes were launched by 3M? Vague needs are the needs we cannot define or pin down, or do not even realize that we have. They are also the needs which arise from new situations presenting unacceptable alternatives – situations in which the decision-makers know what they do *not* want but have not yet been presented with what they *do* want. Whatever people complain about is an indication of a vague need lurking in the psyche. The products which are invented to fulfil vague needs rely very much on inspiration and intuition, and of course, the risks and rewards are very high.

Case 8: A much lesser evil

Although the Romans invented underfloor central heating, throughout most of the last two millennia, householders have struggled to control wood and coal in fireplaces and chimneys. It was a hazardous and dirty method of keeping warm, and it was very hard work. There were other problems too: in cities, coal smoke contributed to dense fog.

The director of a European Building supplies firm often reminds his staff that if people had been told that there was a revolutionary new way of keeping warm, but it involved installing lots of pipework to keep boiling water pumping round their home, and metal eyesores (which would be too hot to touch) in every room, they might have found it quite horrifying. However, once it was established enough in the market for people to be able to make practical comparisons, and assisted by smoke control legislation, water-based central heating became very popular.

Case 9: The need for ultimate accessibility to managing one's finances

Midland Bank was just another UK bank in the late 1980s. Customers were not coming to them expressing what sort of future banking they wanted. In fact, if asked, bank customers might have refused to contemplate the solution Midland were about to develop. Nevertheless, complaints about the lack of accessibility of banks were hitting home – busy people in demanding jobs could not make time to visit the bank when the bank was prepared to be open for business.

Midland set up Project Raincloud, to think about the future of banking. The team came up with the concept of telephone banking. Midland set up a subsidiary called First Direct, the first telephone bank in the UK. It was a great success and took a significant market share in a short period of time.

Case 10: The need for control over information and presentation

In the 1970s, you did not hear managers and professionals saying that they really wanted a machine on their desks which would force them to develop keyboard skills and take on some of the work traditionally done by secretaries or 'techies'. You did hear them complaining that the information they got out of the computer system was not in the right format to facilitate decision-making, it was too little, too late, and if you wanted anything new out of the beast, there was always a two-year programming backlog.

Apple had the vision of ease-of-use desktop computing. Many still regard Apple as the best in desktop computing, even if it is not the most widely used.

Case 11: Getting more out of the garage – you know you want it when you see it

Ann and Carl Sferra of StorageVator Inc. invented their Airflow garage door screens as a response to needs Carl observed when working in a customer's garage installing their storage shelves system for garages.

In order to make full use of their garages, as somewhere to work on the car, or for DIY, or for somewhere to leave pets for short periods, people need the light and ventilation of having the door open, but do not want the insects and dust. The Airflow garage door screen gives them the flexibility they need. Their initial niche market was the golf communities of Florida, where people are on fixed incomes and the regulations of the Home Owners Associations are strict, so affordability and aesthetics were built in.

If people were asked without seeing the product in action whether they knew what would make their garage space more accessible and usable, they might not be able to express it. When they see the product in their neighbour's garage, they know that they want it.

Even when buying decision-makers and consumers are presented with new solutions to solve the problems they did not know could be solved, market researchers still have a considerable challenge in trying to pin down whether consumers' buying intentions will actually be borne out in buying behaviour. The same is true of opinion polls: voting intentions are not always carried through into election results. Researchers would not aspire to picking up aspects of behaviour which only hint at a need, but entrepreneurs have to have the courage to develop products in response to hints of need. The Sony Walkman was based on Akio Morita's observation of his daughter's behaviour which suggested a need to have music with her wherever she went. Prototypes were used by young Japanese celebrities in Tokyo parks to establish whether or not the product would arouse any interest. The rest is history.

Rigorous sanity checking at concept development and prototyping stages is particularly important when companies set out to fulfil vague needs.

Evolving needs

In the case of evolving needs, the supplying company sells the product concept to the customer – all development work takes place within the contract and, because of the length of time involved, the nature of the end product is subject to change.

Customers may start off with a stated need (such as President Kennedy's famous avowed intent to put a man on the moon) but it will be impossible to define how it could be fulfilled, because it has not been fulfilled before. There are many possibilities. By its nature, the need will take years and high levels of speculative experimentation to fulfil. Therefore, as possibilities are explored, the necessary solution can begin to be defined. Innovative engineering projects are renowned for running over time and over budget, disappointing investors, governments and potential customers. This is because the risks are high and there are so many unknowns. Tower Bridge, Concorde and the Channel Tunnel are examples. Where almost unlimited resources are available, such as the Apollo programme, the chances of success are greater.

Evolving needs can also be observed on a smaller scale. Every systems integration and business process redesign project being undertaken in companies today is subject to similar high risk factors, relative to the size of the organization. The degree of newness and change, the length of time to completion and the amount of money involved make such projects difficult to manage. In addition, because of the passage of time, requirements change, and the environment in which the project is executed also changes.

Case 12: A new telecommunications infrastructure for the UK

In the late 1970s, the UK government department responsible for telecommunications engaged a consortium to replace a telephone system based on mechanical Strowger exchanges to an integrated computerized network. They were not able to specify exactly what they wanted from the new system, or any physical or technical characteristics. They had to make decisions on design as technical possibilities were explored. It was a long process of invention, experimentation, adjustment and rigorous testing. It proved to be extremely successful. It facilitated much greater speed and accuracy at lower cost, and the potential for many new telephone services. The result, 'System X', is now almost a commodity product.

Case 13: The fastest route from A to B for a lot of passengers

In the 1960s, the British and French governments poured a lot of money into a plane which would enable supersonic civilian travel. They were not able to specify any materials, capacity, design or technical characteristics. After much experimentation, involving overruns on time and money (common factors in projects to fulfil evolving needs), the result was an engineering triumph called Concorde, which flies 10 miles high at twice the speed of sound (1,350 miles per hour). However, despite the obvious advantages of faster travel over long distances, the future of Concorde is uncertain, as it has proved impossible to reduce the costs to passengers, and the noise associated with supersonic travel has provoked protests from environmental groups.

Case 14: Putting a man on the moon

In 1961, President John F Kennedy announced the Apollo programme to put a man on the moon by the end of the decade. The Apollo 11 mission landed a man on the moon in 1969. The technological feat of a manned moon landing was an end in itself. There was also faith that through this project, the USA would achieve technological breakthroughs which would have valid military and (later) industrial applications. There were many milestones which helped the project to evolve. There were 17 Apollo missions in total, including six follow-up missions after the historic breakthrough.

The choice among competing techniques for achieving a moon landing and return was not made until extensive research had been carried out. There were setbacks, there were even catastrophes, but lessons were learnt and the project marched on. People working on the Apollo programme were inspired by the vision. Psychologists reported that teams with performance ratings in NASA's bottom 50 per cent leapt into the top 15 per cent when they were doing something for the moon programme. Finally, and perhaps decisively, it was accepted that almost unlimited sums of money had to be made available to ensure the success of the project.

Mapping the development challenge

The matrix established in Figure 7.1 enables us to map needs we are fulfilling or planning to fulfil. An example from the information technology industry can illustrate the full application of the matrix and is shown in Figure 7.2.

It is quite usual with high tech companies and capital goods companies to see activity in the vague and evolving boxes. Movement between the boxes can be observed over time. The Internet spent many years in the evolving box before achieving a critical mass of users. It still has to gain mass market acceptance as computer users explore exactly what practical needs it can fulfil, but some functions, such as e-mail, have progressed to the 'specific' box.

Information systems is an industry where the accommodation of the risk associated with breakthrough products is not an option, but an

FIGURE 7.2 Need fulfilment matrix for the information technology industry

Number of users:	Type of use: Straightforward	Difficult to define or multi-faceted concept
Many	SPECIFIC colour printers new software packages new generation PCs 'cut-down' PCs some Internet services	VAGUE computers to reduce domestic chores? combined TV/PC?
Few	BESPOKE network design and implementation	EVOLVING systems integration cross-company business process redesign projects, e.g. supply chain information management
	Lower risk	Higher risk

imperative. It is risky not to take risks. A high tech company without much activity in the vague and evolving boxes would probably have nervous managers.

Companies with top reputations for innovation and developing the next generation of its industry today include 3M, Boeing and JCB. 3M in particular is known for placing strict objectives on sales from new products and enabling staff to indulge in 'pure' research as well as applied research.

It is more difficult to see the opportunities for consumer goods or services companies to work with vague needs to make breakthrough products or services. In the example of the furniture company, it is hard to imagine the transition from vague to specific needs, after all, people have always needed something to sit on. So, let's revisit our historical review.

Were people expressing a need for do-it-yourself furniture? Who on earth would have thought that you could sell sane people a pack of plastic veneered chipboard panels and a few instructions and they would go away happy? People were just expressing dissatisfaction with the cost of furniture and long lead times. So, a new concept emerged, and the problems it presented were considered a reasonable trade-off against the problems it solved.

Were people expressing the need for 'alternative' furniture such as plastic, glass, stripped pine, bean bags and floor cushions? No, but there was a new market segment emerging that thought traditional furniture was unexciting and uninspiring. So, another furniture concept emerged (and left its mark – one of the nominees for the 1997 Turner Prize was 'an interactive bean bag sculpture'!)

Another more recent transition of vague to specific needs is a process one. In the 1970s, people only shopped from catalogues if they lived in remote rural areas. In the 1990s more people are shopping from television, magazines, catalogues and the Internet rather than visiting retail outlets, because it offers more choice and convenience. In the USA, shopping by television and the Internet is a rapidly growing channel to market. So, the new concept which emerges from the vague box need not be a new generation of *products*, it may be new *processes* for accessing or enjoying established products.

The XYZ+20 team can start to map some of their ideas for future products in the matrix resulting in Figure 7.3.

This initial view is helpful, but the team decide to explore possible furniture solutions of the future in more detail. They take a possibility-led approach followed by a reconciliation to the needs-led approach.

FIGURE 7.3   Need fulfilment matrix for XYZ Furniture

	Type of use: Straightforward	Difficult to define or multi-faceted concept
Number of users:		
Many	SPECIFIC furniture adapted for elderly home/office furniture shopping by catalogue, Internet, etc.	VAGUE substitutes for wood + foam aromatherapy furniture 'ergonomics' new fabrics 'lifestyle' concepts 'themed' furniture
Few	BESPOKE hotel furnishing office furnishing	EVOLVING
	Lower risk	Higher risk

Possibility-led approach

What are the product and process probabilities, bearing in mind the future themes identified in Chapter 6? If the project team broke into three sub-groups and brainstormed this topic for half an hour, a list of up to 100 ideas would not be surprising. Using the SCAMPER checklist might result in even more.

The following checklist shows all the ways to vary current products which might be explored.

- Substitute, subtract, split, supplement;

- Combine, cannibalize, circumvent, caricature;

- Adapt, adjoin, align, augment;

- Magnify, minimize, multiply, merge;

- Put to other uses;

- Eliminate, elaborate, else (where else, who else, etc.);

- Rearrange/reconfigure, reverse, refine, revive.

Consider the following examples of ways in which these variations could be implemented.

- *Substitute:*
  - plastic components for metal
  - papier maché for wood
  - air for foam
  - plastic for cloth, etc.

- *Subtract – take out function:*
  - chairs without armrests
  - drawers without handles
  - wardrobes without doors
  - tables without legs, etc.

- *Split – one product into two:*
  - three seater into two seater plus chair
  - wardrobe into hanging units and shelves/cubes for folded items
  - sets of drawers into drawers and frame, etc.

- *Supplement – add options:*
  - footrest to chair
  - umbrella to table
  - cold air to cupboard
  - warm air to cupboard, etc.

- *Combine – two products together:*
  - sofa + bed
  - cupboard + table
  - chair + cupboard/storage space

- *Cannibalize – take something from one product and use in another:*
  - drawers in tables, sofas, beds . . .
  - cushioned table top, etc.

- *Circumvent – a different approach to a function:*
  - chair adjustable for person's leg length
  - non-furniture (sit on boxes), etc.

- *Caricature – make a product feature more pronounced:*
  - big, winged headrests
  - tree trunk style table legs, etc.

- *Adapt – do something in a different way:*
  - water chair
  - blow-up chair
  - blow-up storage space, etc.

- *Adjoin – physically adding something on:*
  - chairs which clip together to form sofa
  - bed plus breakfast table, etc.

- *Align – product synergy with something else:*
  - cupboards for televisions, etc.

- *Augment – add functions:*
  - 'themed' extra covers (for parties, Christmas, etc.)
  - orthopaedic chairs
  - more washability, etc.

- *Magnify – make some/all aspects of the product bigger:*
  - wider chairs, because people are getting bigger
  - longer beds, because people are getting taller, etc.

- *Minimize – make some/all aspects of the product smaller:*
  - miniature furniture for children, etc.

- *Multiply – add more of the same:*
  - extra soft chairs
  - extra hard wearing covers
  - 'nest' of coffee tables
  - incremental cupboard units, etc.

- *Merge – add concepts together for multi-purpose solution:*
  - slats of wood which can fold to make a chair, a table or a case, etc.

- *Put to other uses – same product, new applications:*
  - indoor/outdoor
  - home office furniture, etc.

- *Eliminate – think about obsolete function to take out:*
  - take springs out of chairs and sofas, etc.

- *Elaborate – enhance with more detail:*
  - more craftsmanship
  - better ergonomics
  - more carvings, etc.

- *Else (where else, who else, etc.) – new customers, new channels?:*
  - Internet
  - television

- young people
- magazines, etc.

■ *Rearrange/reconfigure – take existing elements and re-work them:*
  - reconfigurable things to sit on
  - reconfigurable storage units, etc.

■ *Reverse – opposite products or functions:*
  - bed of nails
  - see-through cupboards, etc.

■ *Refine – improve by design, aesthetics:*
  - van Gogh prints for sofa covers
  - copy classic shapes from other products, e.g. cars
  - employ top designers, etc.

■ *Revive – think about obsolete products which may have new applications:*
  - the commode
  - chaise longe
  - kissing seat, etc.

Exploring all of these themes in more depth would generate many variations on fulfilling home comfort needs. The essential challenge is, how many can be related to needs which customers have now, or may have in the future?

Needs-driven reconciliation

The project team needs to consider the dissatisfactions of today, the likely attitudes of consumers in 20 years' time, and see what new products, services and processes may be required. Let's revisit our actionable themes from the business environment. This gives us fairly strong hints about how customer needs are most likely to develop, and therefore where product innovation is required.

■ Work with safety organizations.

■ Reassure customers that XYZ is implementing the latest safety ideas.

■ Initiatives such as the use of video-conferencing to minimize travel, a distribution fleet run on gas rather than diesel, and examining the potential use of solar energy in the factory should be investigated.

■ Be more directly involved in the collection and distribution of second hand furniture to the needy.

- Develop a detailed contingency plan for recovery from a recession.

- Be the first choice of the older generation.

- Use sub-branding to develop new styles and designs to address several other market segments.

- Produce furniture specifically for small households.

- Demonstrate environmental credentials.

- Incorporate health considerations into products, such as ergonomics and aromatherapy.

- Use technology to make processes better, cheaper and faster.

- Research components like smart fabrics which can warm up or cool down according to the room temperature.

- Address the needs of consumers with an office within their home

- Sell furniture over the Internet.

- Produce more portable, adjustable, versatile and durable furniture for all seasons.

However, what can we deduce about vague customer needs, the hints of dissatisfaction today which may become expressed demands in the future, if only an enterprising supplier can show the consumers a good solution?

We can first of all assume that consumers would like to be even safer and more secure, protected if possible from their own mistakes. In terms of 'classic' ranges, continuous improvement on safety and security features is imperative. We can also assume that a significant proportion of consumers in the future are going to be more interested in where their furniture came from and where it might go after they have finished with it. This might require significant innovation in terms of materials used, sourcing of materials, control of sources of materials, and processes for ensuring that the furniture can be re-used, or broken up and its constituent parts re-cycled. Whilst it is a challenge, it can do the company no harm to be ahead of legislation on this topic, and the investigations might also identify some cost advantages.

Equally, developing an ergonomic range and home/office products seems very likely to be worthwhile.

'Lifestyle' trends are notoriously difficult to judge. If 'baby boomers' are still wearing jeans and listening to The Beatles, does it necessarily mean that they want their sofas to be shaped like the front of a 1960s

Cadillac? Do 'outdoor types' necessarily want chairs covered in waxed cotton? Do sailing enthusiasts necessarily want a bed that can reproduce the swell of the sea? Well, we see that following on from theme parks we have themed restaurants and we might expect 'theming' to have got very much more sophisticated by 2020, even down to the level of individual homes.

This area is very high risk, and would have to be premium priced, but it could be highly profitable. The solution might be a 'furnishings consultancy' whereby hotels, offices or wealthy individuals could specify their own theme for furniture which could then be built to order, providing useful hints for the consumer market along the way. Whether their uniqueness is a matter of special fabrics, special shaping or special technology would be reflected in the price. The 'swell of the sea' bed and similar challenges might even take furniture development into the product development challenges associated with evolving needs.

This kind of analysis helps us with the market overall. It leads on to the question of market segmentation. Can a close look at segmentation give us any indications about where we should focus our efforts?

Market segmentation in the future

As we have already noted, customers are individuals with differing lifestyles and tastes. It is already possible, in 1997, to have enough information about individual's tastes that even our traditional segmentation model may fragment down to a much greater degree of granularity. We can call up at the touch of a button, information about Mrs X, what she buys and what she says she wants. We may even know her buying criteria and why she buys from us rather than the competitors, or vice versa.

In the future, when we ask 'who are the customers?', segmentation will in fact be an aggregation. We will be clustering customers' individual needs, rather than breaking a 'mass' market into sub-sections according to the guidance of market research sampling. The complete picture of the market could be along the lines of a customer portfolio analysis as illustrated in Figure 7.4.

It is still likely that we would find clusters, which we could call segments even though they might not be so neatly generalized as they have been in the past. The larger clusters would facilitate the identification of the most attractive opportunities in the market and the

FIGURE 7.4 Customer portfolio analysis attractiveness vs. performance matrix. Note that the vertical axis runs from right to left. This may seem counter-intuitive, but it is the way the original designers intended it to be. Our focus is concentrated on the top left-hand box. This box is based on the Directional Policy Matrix jointly developed by General Electric and McKinsey.

		Our performance on customers' buying criteria	
	High High	Low	
	Franco Siberini Surinder Kaur		
		Johann Schreyer	
	Jan Janssen Jo Mann		
	Elise Dupont	Charlotte Clarke	
	Les Jones		
	Wolfgang Braun	Maxine Renoir	
Customer attractiveness	Miguel Lopez	Jill Iyles	
		Maggie McLeod	
	Liz Winston		
		Jean Smith	
	Sam Green	John Silverman	
	Michel Chevalier		
	Ron Ricardo	Peter Seitz	
	Low	Bill Peters	
	Eduardo Fernandez	Heinrich Schmidt	
	Peter Branning		

development of core offerings for them. However, if the social trend of increasing individuality and lifestyle diversity does continue, then we ought to conclude that the market leader in the furniture market (and many other consumer markets of the future) will be the company that can excel in the most niche markets. In general, a multi-niche strategy ought to deliver prosperity. But which niches? If we wish to seize the future, whilst hanging on to some traditional strengths, we should use our current segmentation as a starting point.

Segment A

Segment A contains the 'Classics' – reasonably well-off, conservative people, who stick to tried and trusted formulae in home comfort. We have established that this segment has declined, but it seems unlikely that it will ever disappear, and it is important as the company seizes its future that it should stay in touch with its history. The main problem is that it is the easiest segment and therefore one which competitors will also target.

The XYZ Furniture company has been producing classical furniture for many decades, and has strong capabilities in the design and styling for these customers and their specific need of aesthetically pleasing and functional home comforts. Ways of combining manufacturing technology with craftsmanship and providing more and more choice in terms of coverings and configurations, will provide a secure basis for XYZ in the future.

Segment B

Segment B customers are people on low incomes. This group has never been a strategic segment for XYZ. However, if 'green' sentiment revives the second hand market in a significant way, the collection of old furniture and distribution to the appropriate outlets could be a franchise opportunity for XYZ to establish.

Segments C–F

These four segments contain people driven by practicalities; those who have high aspirations; who are fashion conscious; and whose lifestyle drives their buying decisions. All these segments will be subject to degrees of overlap and degrees of fragmentation. For example, in Segment C, the specific practicalities needed by elderly people will require special attention, whilst a 'green', fun or nostalgia theme could appeal to any number of people in Segments E or F.

XYZ Furniture company in 2020

The XYZ+20 project team is coming to the conclusion that market leadership in consumer markets in the future will require a multi-niche approach, as there will be no such thing as a 'mass' market, and no one niche big enough to sustain market leadership over a long period of time. Therefore, XYZ Limited in 2020 could look like this:

- XYZ Classics Division
  Same formula as today but with new coverings and configurations.

- XYZ Logistics (in co-operation with charities)
  Delivery, collection and recycling (fleet operating on bio-fuel!).

- XYZ Green Division
  Environmentally friendly, furniture from recycled sources.

- XYZ Fun Division
  Novelty furniture (such as blow-up cupboards) and fun accessories, such as special covers for furniture for parties.

- XYZ Indoor/outdoor
  Versatile, hardy furniture for a variety of uses and seasons.

- XYZ Nostalgia
  Designs from the past to suit the age of a house or a favourite era.

- XYZ Senior
  Specially adapted furniture, e.g. chairs which lower an elderly person into the seat and which gently tip them forward when they need to get up.

- XYZ Office
  For the office within the home.

- XYZ Global
  Design themes from around the world.

- XYZ Children's Division
  Ultra safe, ultra durable, small furniture.

- XYZ Furniture technology and special effects
  e.g. bed which mimics the swell of the sea, sets of drawers with alarms.

- XYZ Furnishings consultancy
  Knowledge-based approach to companies such as hotels or property agents, or individuals with unique requirements, leading to bespoke manufacturing of their preferred solution.

- XYZ Head Office
  Providing common mission, strategic framework, finance, information technology, and human resource expertise for the whole group. Also responsible for relationships with major retailers and other key accounts, e.g. hotels, department store chains.

This means, in terms of the market map, that the company as a whole would be operating in every corner of the market. The sub-brands which will be needed for each niche may use different outlets, and may require different sources of supply.

In a 3–5 year outlook, I would suggest that the planning team might not have been so adventurous. The programme required to implement this future view will build up over a longer period, unless growth by acquisition is a feasible option. In the meantime, since we cannot really cross the 'I's and dot the 'T's on a 20–30 year outlook, the project team might feel that further detail would be spurious detail. This is after all, only one solution. It needs to be subjected to some creative reconstruction, which will follow in the next chapter.

Now our review of the most probable future is complete. We made our choice, as XYZ Furniture company, to:

- recognize consumer power and demand for lifestyle choices;

- recognize the specific practical needs of different age groups;

- make an opportunity out of increasing trends to shop and work from home;

- build on current strengths but meet the challenge to enter new niche markets;

- provide for corporate customers as well as consumers;

- investigate aspects of new technology which could fulfil customer needs.

SUMMARY

In this chapter, we have established:

- how an analysis of different types of need can help innovation;

- reconciled a possibility-led and needs-led approach to defining the products and processes of the future;

- considered the changing nature of segmentation and the power of information about customers;

- established the company's need to enter new segments if it is to achieve market leadership;

- considered what that might look like.

In Chapter 8, we play some mind games to ensure we have embraced all possibilities, and to establish what contingency plans might be needed.

CHAPTER EIGHT

Practising abstract thinking techniques to test the most likely scenario

Murder boarding

A mouse never trusts its life to a single hole.

Plautus

Of course, our cautiously optimistic view of the future will be interrupted in some way by events. John Leslie, Canadian philosopher and author of *The End of the World* estimates that there is a 5 per cent chance that the world will be destroyed in the next 500 years. If it happens within the period of your plan, you won't need to worry about not having anticipated it.

Doomsday scenarios need only concern us as a way of testing our scenario. They may be stepping stones to improving it, or identifying shrewd contingency plans. We need contingency plans for the business, just as we need them in our own lives. In order to stimulate our thinking about such contingencies, we can use a variety of abstract techniques, starting with 'murder boarding' our business environment. Then using reversal and re-reversal, analogies, random combinations and role play, our future view of the company can be put through its paces.

Murder boarding the most likely business environment

Sometimes the project team have to ask colleagues to get together to destroy their well-crafted plan. Murder boarding is a negative application of brainstorming. It requires the team to think of everything that is wrong with something. As a coffee break exercise, I often ask people attending workshops to choose a product they hate and murder board it in their syndicate groups. They think it is great fun, even when they know that the next exercise is to think of ways to make the product better. The top favourites are supermarket trolleys, electric hand dryers, mobile phones and car alarms. No one ever chooses one of their own companies' products!

The reason for this is that it is very difficult for us to criticize things which are dear to us. Thus it is advisable for the project team to leave their chosen colleagues in a sound-proofed room to murder board the scenario they have spent days building. After the outpouring of 'gut feel' criticism, the murder boarders have to work on justifying their criticisms and making constructive suggestions to resolve them, which they then present back to the project team.

Doomsday scenarios

The review team might start off by listing every possible doomsday scenario in order to establish which contingency plans are required. Consider the following seven scenarios.

- *Meteorite hits earth.* Well, highly unlikely but perhaps we do need to have a contingency plan in the event of a major disaster hitting a strategic source of supply, or our own facilities. Wood dust is highly combustible, and in the past fire was a regular hazard in every furniture factory. Besides accidents and error, sabotage is a growing threat in some other industries, such as the food industry, and anything to do with animals.

- *Competitors discover home furnishings equivalent of Superman's krypto-nite.* What if the competitors make a technological breakthrough? One answer is that there is nothing wrong with being a fast follower. IBM did not produce the world's first commercial computers, but they came to dominate the market. IBM did not produce the world's first personal computers, but established the standard hardware platform. Even if the company endorses the project team's strategic outlook, they might still require advance plans for future tactical responses to competitor activity. In the furniture industry, it may even be feasible to adopt a strategy of waiting for a market entrant to develop a niche market and then acquire the company to develop XYZ's portfolio.

- *Psychologically unbalanced dictator gains power in a major economy and there is a war.* If there is a protracted war involving countries where we operate, we might expect a return to the rationing of consumer goods, or at least a 'feel-bad' factor which will result in self-rationing. All competitors will be equally affected. Survival will depend on the capability to quickly wind down production.

- *Politicians panic and resort to economic protectionism.* Who can really be sure that all the world's political leaders have learnt from the mistakes that were made in the 1930s? Despite the efforts of GATT, there are still elements of protectionism in the world economy. There is a small risk that protectionism may re-emerge in a substantial way. It could have almost the same effect as war.

- *From pack animals to alone in the lair.* There is a view that, just as economic and technological progress enabled the transition from the extended family living together to the nuclear family as a household unit, we are now seeing a transition to lone adult living. This is excellent news for us. There will be more households and more furniture. However, for most of their lives lone adults are not nest building, some never nest build. Their drive for home comforts may be minimal.

- *Non-shopping takes off.* There could be a backlash against the consumer society – see war and economic protectionism, as the effect would be similar.

- *Killer bug lurks in the living room.* There is always a possibility that an influenza epidemic or some new plague will decimate customer numbers. Science fiction writers and journalists earn money exploring the consequences. The effects on business would be the same as a meteorite or war. What if the killer bug were closely associated with XYZ furniture? Perhaps we should take more note of insurance industry warnings that companies are under-insured against many risks, including negligence claims, pollution, health and safety issues, computer bugs, etc.

As the team goes on, they become more convinced of the very marginal levels of probability they are dealing with. Nevertheless, three reasonable messages have emerged.

- The home furnishings industry is particularly vulnerable to adverse economic or market circumstances and a survival plan should be prepared.

- Does XYZ have to take the risk of being an innovator? XYZ could be a fast follower or buy up innovative start-up companies. The project team should offer decision-makers a 'market leadership by stealth' option.

- Disaster planning needs to be constantly revisited and refined, and new risks incorporated.

XYZ+20 is already committed to the first finding, as long as it is accompanied by a robust plan for a quick-start recovery from recession, and we would agree that the final message is a good idea. The second finding generates some debate, with the review team quoting recent articles about Microsoft's approach to innovation – by acquisition. The project team accept it as a contingency plan if investment funds are not sufficient to sustain the main scenario.

Murder boarding the 2020 position for XYZ

The second stage is to murder what the project team have specifically assumed about the business environment. The review must be provocative – acting as 'devil's advocate' to test the robustness of the emerging strategy. More than one angle of criticism may be explored for each item; twelve suggestions follow.

- *Safety.* There is a limit to how much suppliers can protect customers from their own cigarette ends, DIY incompetence, or clumsy pets and children. Employing top lawyers and lobbyists to vigorously defend the industry from further safety legislation would be more cost-effective.

- *Environment.* The green lobby has had its day. Any movement which promotes some vision of purity will eventually come up against the frailties of the vast majority of the population. People in mature democracies vote in favour of their own comforts.

- *Modest economic growth.* There is always some part of the world which has high growth rates, why not seek them out and relocate there! Alternatively, boom and bust may get more accentuated.

- *Nostalgic baby boomers.* Baby boomers may still wear jeans, but their homes eventually tend to look much like their parents'.

- *Brand driven young consumers.* Whilst they are playing with their parents' money young consumers are brand-conscious. However when they start having to pay the bill for brands themselves, discounters will get a new lease of life!

- *Fear of crime.* By the time customers have finished fitting their homes with alarms and cameras, nothing will need to be added to furniture. Just find some way of making sure customers keep their receipts for the insurance claim.

- *Family variations.* There could be a huge backlash to current changing life styles. Governments may use the benefits system to force people back into nuclear or extended families.

- *Health.* People will get tired of the health lobby. Who wants to live to 120 anyway? Alternatively, people will want to be so healthy they won't be sitting down for long, so will value their furniture less.

- *Internet sales.* If only the Internet really worked. But even if it did, people will get fed up of having technology forced down their throats and will go and find people to talk to when they want to buy something.

- *Mixing shop floor technology with craftsmanship.* Why should XYZ worry about trying to blend technology and craftsmanship? Either invest in technology or import from where skilled labour is cheap.

- *Telecommuting.* There will always be people will not want to miss out on office gossip, and managers will not want to lose control, so even telecommuting will have a limited effect.

- *Better weather.* The jury is still out on global warming. Weather patterns may yet reverse.

The review team and the project team then need to work together to establish whether the most likely scenario needs revision, or whether any given point made is major enough to demand a contingency plan. The two teams must reach consensus on the impact which any of the alternatives might have, and its relative probability of occurrence (Figure 8.1).

For example, XYZ+20 and their review team decide on the mapping of potential contingency occurrences shown in Figure 8.2. The review team and project team would probably decide to concentrate their debate on the top left-hand box, and resolve just to note the other items.

- *To go green or not to go green* – Should XYZ have a 'green' division, if the influence of the green lobby might diminish? Even if the mass membership and political influence of environmental charities decreased, might it not still constitute a viable niche market? In

FIGURE 8.1   Probability matrix

| | Probability of occurrence | |
	High	Low
High	Incorporate in main scenario if considered more probable than current outlook, or make a contingency plan.	Contingency plan?
Impact on the workability of the whole scenario	Contingency plan?	No action
Low		

FIGURE 8.2   Probability matrix – XYZ Furniture

| | Probability of occurrence | |
	High	Low
High	Green movement loses momentum Baby boomers join 'classics' *en masse* People get fed up of technology	Relocate to higher growth economies Telecommuting does not take off
Impact on the workability of the whole scenario	Backlash against lone living Backlash against health lobby	Anti-safety lobby Weather worsens
Low		

many consumer markets, where companies have established environmental and ethical credentials, they have achieved worthwhile market share. Could XYZ get into the game if elsewhere in the division, sister companies were offering leather sofas and mahogany tables?

It is agreed that XYZ should concentrate on promoting recycling as its contribution to the environment. In any event, if the company as a whole cannot claim 'purity', then it is pointless to try to set up a division on that basis. The technology division can research whether environmental improvements can be built into all products, and the 'novelty' division might offer some green themes.

- *To go lifestyle or to stick with classics* – The problem with sticking with classics is that every competitor wants to do that. It is the easy option. Even if they just want some small degree of individuality about their products, consumers deserve a choice. XYZ+20 are committed to staying with classics, but also believe that XYZ must research lifestyle niches carefully, and make sure it occupies a critical mass of them.

- *To surf the Net or not to surf the Net* – Some people may get fed up of it, some will not. Already 21 per cent of American households use the Internet regularly, for purposes which include buying consumer goods. Its usability is bound to improve as time marches on. By 2020, it will be combined with television and telephony; it cannot be ignored. Provided that XYZ continues to supply retail outlets, fluctuations in the popularity of channels should be accommodated.

The review team have come up with some valid points, but concede that the project team are still 'on track'. Now the two teams have to mix themselves up and split into smaller sub-teams to try the abstract thinking techniques which will test possibilities further.

Applying abstract techniques to the outlook for customer needs and XYZ solutions

The ground rules for idea generation sessions (see Chapter 3) apply to all these exercises.

Reversal/re-reversal

If an opposite seems absurd, the value of a proposal can be more vividly appreciated and its features developed. Reversal/re-reversal can also generate new possibilities. Can you reverse the need you fulfil and come up with something new to do? Can you reverse the solution you offer to shed new light on it? If, in the pursuit of vague needs to fulfil, you do not know what the customer wants, can you determine what the customer does not want, suggest solutions and then reverse them?

The Post-it note was developed by a chemist at 3M practising this technique – he was researching very strong glues, so he experimented with very weak ones. The control of noise on some aircraft is achieved through the production of anti-noise, i.e. sound waves which interfere with those of the original noise.

This is a mind-bending exercise, but very popular with groups who have used it, especially in those industries where technology or services have moved very rapidly, sometimes leaving original concepts about 'need' in limbo. It genuinely enables some deep thought about the meaning of customer needs and proposed solutions. From this deliber-ately orchestrated confusion, some companies have been able to start to work out a number of new angles on potential future customer needs and solutions to fulfil them. The reason it works is because we are in fact slightly twisting the concept every time we try to turn it on its head and back again, so we get restatements which challenge our assumptions. In order to show its effect, three examples are considered – furniture, security systems and transport. Table 8.1 identifies needs fulfilled by these three industries.

The first step is to reverse the need that the product fulfils and brainstorm products to fulfil the reversed need. Table 8.2 lists the reversed needs for our three industries

Column 3 of Table 8.2 contains some very plausible concepts, because the need to stay put can be just as obvious as the need to travel. In column 2, however, it might appear that absurdity rules, until you talk

TABLE 8.1 Consumer need fulfilment by industry

Industry	Furniture	Security systems	Transport
Needs fulfilled	Comfort and tidiness in the home	Exclusion of unwanted persons	Getting people from A to B

TABLE 8.2   Reversed consumer needs

Industry	Furniture	Security systems	Transport
Reversed need	Home discomfort and untidiness	Encourage unwelcome persons	Keep people at A
Solutions to reversed need:	■ Lumpy sofa ■ Badly fitting cupboards ■ Chairs with different leg lengths (rocking chair!) ■ Narrow chairs with no legroom (like aircraft seats!) ■ Bed of nails ■ Sloping shelves ■ See-through cupboards ■ Noisy chairs ■ Short hanging space in wardrobes	■ Neon sign 'something to rob here' ■ Open all doors and windows ■ Widely available telephone number ■ Jewellery hanging from the curtains ■ Darkness ■ Invite any passer-by round for drinks ■ Direct mail to prisons ■ Leaflet outside courts	■ Video-conferencing ■ Straight-jacket ■ Prison ■ Curfew ■ Telephone ■ Fax ■ E-mail ■ Tele-commuting ■ Virtual reality ■ Good television ■ DIY

to police officers about some of the carelessness they come across. We might expect more from this when we re-reverse. In column 1, there is a combination of absurd ideas with some products already in existence and others with potential. The rocking chair may have started out as an accident! Cupboards with see-through doors are more commonly known as display cabinets. Have another look at 'lumpy sofa'. Why do people buy seat covers of wooden beads for their cars? Perhaps they would like the same effect at home? Also think about 'noisy chairs': could we develop cocoon-style chairs including options for soothing music?

The second step in the reversal/re-reversal process is to brainstorm a list of reversals of the concept of current products (Table 8.3).

Terrorists, vandals, thieves and other criminals know only too well how to stop transport functioning, so column 3 in Table 8.3 looks familiar. Column 2 offers little which may lead to new lines of enquiry –

TABLE 8.3 Reversals of the concepts of current products

Industry	Furniture	Security systems	Transport
Function	Something to sit on or in Something to put things on or in	Physical blocking mechanisms, such as locks; alarms	Personal transport: cars, bicycles, etc. 'Public' transport: Buses/trains/planes
Reversals	■ Something to sit under ■ Something to put things under ■ Something to take things out of ■ Something to get out of ■ Something to force you to stand ■ Something that lets things fall out	■ Physical access mechanism ■ Silent alarm ■ Alarm that goes off when no burglar ■ Force field to pull people in	■ Remove wheels ■ Remove engines, gears ■ Sabotage traffic lights ■ Sabotage rail signals ■ Sabotage air traffic control

could the silent alarm be a shock wave within the violated territory? In Column 1, there is little to tempt our intrepid project team, except that something to help the elderly up from their chairs leads on from one or two of the angles listed. Sometimes, it happens that way.

The third step is to reverse/restate the outcome of the first step. Suggested solutions for our three industries are shown in Table 8.4. Here we can see how difficult it is to truly 'reverse' everything. Some of the restatements do not make sense, but every idea must have its space, in case it leads another member of the team to build from it to something which does make sense, as in the case of the bears and snow on the lines. Column 3 of Table 8.4 perhaps emphasizes how much more important transport must be in a free democracy than in a restricted society. Column 2 emphasizes how simple measures might help people to achieve the security they want. 'Direct mail from prisons' reflects demands communities make on police authorities to know who the criminals are in their midst. Column 1 raises the question for our furniture company project team 'How good are we at producing good quality furniture?' This might be very relevant for ensuring continued success in the 'classics'.

TABLE 8.4 Solutions to reversed needs, re-reversed

Industry	Furniture	Security systems	Transport
Solutions to reversed need, re-reversed	■ Smooth sofa ■ Well-fitting cupboards ■ Chairs with identical leg lengths ■ Wide chairs with legroom ■ Bed supported by nails ■ Straight shelves ■ Closeted cupboards ■ Quiet chairs ■ Long hanging space in wardrobes	■ Neon sign 'nothing to rob here' ■ Shut all doors and windows ■ Private telephone number ■ Jewellery hidden away ■ Light ■ Invite no passer-by round for drinks ■ Direct mail from prisons ■ Leaflet inside courts	■ Telepathy ■ Unfettered people ■ Free people ■ Out any time ■ Letters ■ Communicate in person ■ Physical commuting ■ Reality ■ Bad television ■ Get someone else in to do it

The final step is to reverse/restate the reversed need which started the exercise. In Table 8.5, Column 3, our somewhat restated need has inspired a more pro-active approach, the team has moved on to consider how to generate more travel. In Column 2, preventing unwelcome visitors has progressed to repelling unwelcome persons. In Column 1, with our age-old concept of furniture, we are confined to perfecting it. Nevertheless, this in itself is helpful guidance.

Analogy

Analogy is a way of thinking through what the business is like. How is this customer need fulfilled in other environments? I have likened hotels to bee-hives. There is a lot of resting, feeding and cleaning going on in bee-hives. Think some more about bee-hives and consider whether the differentiator for hotels in the future might be the quality of its security. Worker bees will die before letting strangers into the hive.

Even if the analogy is not direct, reframing the business in another setting can provide breakthrough inspiration. Nature is the richest source

TABLE 8.5 Restatement of initial reversed need

Industry	Furniture	Security systems	Transport
Reversed need	Home discomfort and untidiness	Encourage unwelcome persons	Keep people at A
Re-reversal	Home comfort and tidiness	Discourage unwelcome persons	Send people from A
New angles to re-reversed need	■ Emphasis on quality of workmanship ■ Ensure sofas, beds, etc. tested for support	■ Emit unpleasant smells or sensations when uninvited persons approach	■ Drive people out by bad television ■ Provide travel offers (e.g. rail + meal) ■ Travel points schemes ■ Provide incentives to employers to send staff all over the country

of analogy. Millions of years of evolution can normally be relied upon for good solutions to needs. Domestic situations, and cross-fertilization with other professions, have also made significant contributions to technological progress. Consider the following examples of what inspired what.

- *New lining for furnaces – bird's nests.* As a result of a creativity exercise, a product development team decided on a clay lining for a new furnace, after considering the virtues of the way birds use mud to line their nests.

- *Anglepoise lamp – human arm.* The inventor of the anglepoise lamp recreated what might happen if someone working at a desk had a servant to adjust the light source for them.

- *Spitfire fighter aircraft – seagulls.* The inventor of the Spitfire fighter aircraft was inspired by the swooping of seagulls.

- *'Cats' eyes' in road markings – real cats' eyes.* The inventor of the little lights in road markings actually named his product after its inspiration.

- *Telephone – human ear.* The technology of the telephone mimics what happens in a human ear. The telephone system is an ear magnified millions of times.

- *Velcro – seed burrs.* The properties of Velcro are directly modelled on seed burrs.

- *Snoring cure – aircraft wings.* A cure for some types of snoring was derived from aircraft wing technology. Surgeons from Addenbrookes Hospital in Cambridge got together with engineers from Peterhouse College. The engineers were used to the concept of thickening soft materials to reduce vibration. One of the surgeons noticed that scarring made throat tissue thicker. Scar tissue can be created by laser. By June 1994, 50 patients with snoring problems had been helped by operations involving laser scarring of throat tissue.

- *New road humps – breast implants.* Technology and materials borrowed from plastic surgery are being applied to reduce the noise and jolting problems inherent in solid humps.

- *Pasteurization – fermentation.* A classic example of the partial analogy, it was Pasteur's observation of fermenting grapes which enhanced his understanding of infection and led to his solution to it.

- *Sony Walkman – daughter's behaviour.* Akio Morita noticed that his daughter wanted music wherever she went, so he invented a product which would allow her to achieve this.

- *New glass making process – washing-up.* The process involved in this common domestic chore inspired improved quality in glass making at Pilkington.

- *Computer disk packaging – scuba diving.* An IBM engineer applied a principle from his hobby of scuba diving to develop safe packaging for sensitive computer disks.

- *Self-operating vacuum cleaner – trilobite.* The latest breakthrough in vacuum cleaning was inspired by an arthropod which lived in the sea millions of years ago. It survived by crawling along the ocean bed sucking up debris.

- *Airlines – Formula 1.* Process benchmarking also makes use of analogy. Dallas-based South West Airlines looked outside the airline industry in order to perfect its refuelling processes. Using the turnaround processes used in pit stops in Formula 1 motor racing, the time required to refuel was reduced by 60 per cent.

- *Electricity company processes – parcels delivery.* Scottish Power compared every aspect of its processes with utilities in other parts of the world with special challenges (such as maintaining power in the typhoon belt) and with other companies such as Federal Express for customer service.

Once again, we will work with a number of examples, including furniture, in our exploration of the help to be derived from seeking analogies, so that a variety of outcomes can be observed.

Bearing in mind the three industries we used earlier – furniture, security systems and transport – we will consider in Table 8.6 how animals and plants fulfil their needs for:

- home comforts;

- security;

- moving around.

From our transport analogies we observe the famous inspiration for air travel – animal flight. The hovering ability of a humming bird has been incorporated into a design for a flying car. Engineers are still trying to learn from the miracles associated with the flight of insects. We have also identified some marvellous new possibilities for security systems.

For furniture, XYZ+20 have to work a little harder to spot learning points. Have the possibilities of ceramics in furniture been fully explored (mud in bird's nests)? Do we supply as much ornamentation as people would like (jackdaws)? Should furniture be made to look more natural (arrangements of stones)? Should traditional stuffings be used instead of foam? Should we investigate the appeal of hexagons (bees)? If cars seats can be heated, why not heat beds and sofas directly? In fact, smart fabrics which can warm or cool the occupant of a chair according to ambient temperature are expected to be available within 10–20 years.

Combinations

Many companies successfully use recombinations to develop their product line, but concentrate their item lists around their existing product range. Rubbermaid, the households products manufacturer which is one of the most admired companies in the USA, have a number of recombination

TABLE 8.6   Nature's solutions to identified consumer needs

Industry	Furniture	Security systems	Transport
Needs fulfilled	Comfort and tidiness in the home	Exclusion of unwanted creatures	Getting from A to B
Nature's equivalent	■ Nests, made with twigs, mud and feathers ■ Jackdaws alleged to decorate with shiny things ■ Adapt natural features, e.g. arrangement of stones ■ Padding with dried vegetation or fur/hair ■ Bees store in hexagonal wax chambers ■ Keep warm in own body fat	■ Bees – kill or be killed ■ Skunks – emit smell ■ Toads – emit poison ■ Porcupines – use spines ■ Cats – mark territory with urine ■ Skuas – kick ■ Fulmars – vomit ■ Chameleons – change colour	■ Seed burrs travel on host (animal fur) ■ Some seed pods explode, catapulting seeds some distance ■ Seeds travel through animals who eat them ■ Animals hitch lifts on other animals ■ Spiders swing on their own web ■ Some fly ■ Some swim ■ Some run very fast

options. For example – in order to save space in the garage you can buy a Rubbermaid stepping stool which doubles up as a tool box.

Other companies conceptually combine current solutions with some apparently unrelated thing to develop a revolutionary potential for their product line. Product breakthroughs are often combinations of known things. For example, the inventor of the printing press said that he had combined the concepts of a coin punch and a wine press to create his revolutionary machine. The teasmade is a combination of a clock and a kettle. An Icelandic farmer combined a cow byre with a café and created a unique tourist attraction. For some time now, UK supermarkets have been providing banking services. Who or what might you combine with in order to be better equipped to meet consumers' future needs?

In order to come up with new product ideas, remembering that quantity is the first priority, the product development team can work on forced recombinations. This exercise should be familiar, as it is often used by primary school teachers. To ask children to write a story or draw a picture involving apparently unrelated objects, such as a dragon, a box and an umbrella, develops their imagination as much as their writing or drawing skills.

The procedure is quite simple. To start, the team brainstorms two lists of objects, which may or may not be relevant to the product range – fifteen in each would be sufficient. The facilitator then pairs items at random and asks teams of two to come up with ways in which the pair might be linked to create something useful.

For example, in one exercise, team members linked car and slug and came up with:

- apply the clinging power of a slug to tyre technology to prevent skidding

- produce cars that glide along the road

- use cars to kill slugs

Believe it or not, a car concept called 'the slug' appeared at last year's UK motor show!

Now XYZ+20 have to try the same for furniture:

LIST A	LIST B
chair	food
table	slug
bed	bell
bedside cabinet	sword
Welsh dresser	shoe
bookcase	tank
kitchen units	car
sofa	radiator
cupboard	flower
stool	glass
wardrobe	switch
lamp stand	exercise
coffee table	streetlight
desk	calendar
filing cabinet	toilet
shelves	window

Possible combinations might be:

- chair with integral food tray for TV dinners (like the front seats in aircraft)

- chairs and sofas with glide mechanism rather than castors to avoid marks on the carpet

- chairs with foot warmers rather than foot rests

- Welsh dresser with integral fish tank

- heated sofas and chairs

- bedside cabinets with built in alarm clock

- furniture plus aromatherapy

- desk with integral calendar/personal organizer

- chair + toilet – the commode again!

- office chair combined with exercise machine

- bookcase for bathrooms

XYZ+20 have found some reasonable areas for further research and some novelty possibilities.

Role play

The final test for our confidence in the future is role play: an approach said to be at the heart of the genius of physicist Richard Feynman was his ability to ask himself 'If I were an electron, what would I do?' I would suggest that it is the mark of business genius to ask: 'If I were a customer, what would I feel?' In my last book I mentioned the story of John Spiers, a successful businessman who became Chairman of the Brighton Health Care Trust. He took to a wheelchair to test the service he was in charge of providing. He went through fear, extreme cold and indignity when he set out to discover 'the invisible hospital – the one patients experience but which the managers never see.'

The Managing Director of a UK travel company was recently filmed taking on the role of a travel representative for his own company in a Spanish holiday destination. He found out what life was like for one of his 'front-line troops', and observed at first hand why customers complain and what they complain about.

The XYZ+20 team trek round a variety of furniture stores as mystery shoppers and observers of real shoppers, to get some inspiration for this exercise.

When XYZ+20 envisage the world of 2020, they are initially doing so from the point of view of a company that wants to be the market leader in its industry in 2020. This, of course, can only happen if customers are prepared to buy its products. So, before we consider what aspects of our future scenario are robust enough to include in shorter term planning, we must get inside the minds of future customers. Some companies employ actors to help project team members think themselves into roles.

Whether or not professional help is available, we can help ourselves by starting close to home.

- *Ourselves as customers* – What are we like as customers now, compared to our behaviour in the 1970s? Have we become more demanding? Most consumers have. Each individual might have a different approach to present to the team. Usually, like Lottery winners, consumers swear to market researchers that '*x* will not change my life'. But behaviour does change over time. As scenario gazers, the project team might be better placed than most to predict how their behaviour will change and how that will affect the way they buy furniture.

  All our own dissatisfactions and vague needs can be explored. Will our scenario really address them? Most creative executives yearn for the easy chair plus exercise bike that enables them to keep fit whilst finishing off a report at home!

- *Customers observed in the mystery shopping exercise* – Can team members really relate to the furniture buyers they observed in their retail walkabout? It is worth trying! What were they asking about? What problems did they want to solve?

- *Customers from hell* – The team can have enormous fun role-playing the sort of customers who go to extremes to test the capabilities of the company. Inspiration for these roles often comes from comic television personalities, such as the Solomon Family in *Third Rock From the Sun*, who are really aliens and expose all the absurdities of human behaviour; and the hilarious grumpiness of the BBC's Victor 'I simply don't believe it!' Meldrew. Funny though it is, the arch complainers of the 1970s are representative of the average consumer of the 1990s, so what can the future hold? Durability and quality gain focus here!

- *Children* – What will the children we know today be like as consumers in their thirties? Members of the team should present to their team mates a particular child they know, how they behave now and how they might behave in the future. The computer enthusiast, the brand freak, the coach potato and the keen interrogator about ingredients and E-numbers will probably all be there. Can our scenario stand up to their scrutiny? Watching toy craze after toy craze, adults tend to assume that the children we know will want themed home comforts when they are consumers for the first time. If home furnishing fashion starts to change as quickly as toys, trainers and football strips, offerings might have to be very inexpensive.

- *Inanimate objects* – A very successful formula for a new shampoo was supposedly derived from a team sitting together to discuss 'what I would want if I were a split end'. A headline grabbing advertising campaign for a certain coffee brand was alleged to have resulted from a team asking themselves 'How I would want to be advertised if I were a coffee bean?' So our furniture project team ought to ask themselves: 'If I were a tree, growing today for harvest in 2020, what would I want to be?' (If the answer is 'still alive', explore the concept of living furniture – thus combining house plants with things to sit on or put things on.) Ask 'if I were a house in 2020, what would I want inside me?' and so on.

This last variation, even with a market as long established as the furniture market, may throw up some revolutionary ideas.

At the end of these abstract exercises we have to decide:

- Have we revised our view of customer needs, or proposed solutions?

- Have we more confidence in the main scenario?

So far it appears that our furniture team, XYZ+20, have established the nature of the furniture industry is such that many ways of developing the current product range seem trivial or gimmicky. However, given that the examples shown are only a fraction of those that might be developed in the time available to the project team, we have nevertheless established that:

- there is potential for innovation even with the classics, e.g. integral heating, glide mechanisms, ergonomic testing for comfort/support;

- there is plenty of potential for development of lifestyle and novelty furniture (such as living furniture);

- a furniture technology division might be able to identify much more.

Our main scenario can progress, with the exception of the 'green' division, murdered in the review. Meanwhile, contingency plans must be developed for surviving some kind of major economic or market disaster, and for 'fast following' rather than innovation. In short:

XYZ Furniture Company in 2020 – main scenario

- XYZ Classics Division
- XYZ Logistics & recycling
- XYZ Fun Division
- XYZ Indoor/outdoor
- XYZ Nostalgia
- XYZ Senior
- XYZ Office
- XYZ Global
- XYZ Children's Division
- XYZ Furniture technology and special effects
- XYZ Furnishings consultancy

XYZ Furniture Company in 2020 – survival scenario

- XYZ Classics Division

Basic functional designs, modelled on the 'utility' furniture available during the Second World War.

XYZ Furniture Company in 2020 – fast follower scenario

- XYZ Classics Division
- XYZ Logistics & recycling
- XYZ Acquisitions:
  - Novelty furniture – whatever a start-up company can make a market for
  - Conservatory/Outdoor
  - Senior
  - Office
  - Children's

SUMMARY

In this chapter we have:

■ asked a review team to murder board the most likely scenario;

■ identified the potential for contingency plans;

■ used abstract techniques to gain new insights into possible customer needs and potential solutions;

■ tested our confidence in the main scenario.

In Chapter 9, we tackle the tricky subject of how to start implementing the project team's ideas.

CHAPTER NINE

Managing implementation

Implementing the scenario

> Most companies . . . develop great strategies, but implement few of them because, like many slimmers, they lack the willpower. It takes courage to enforce strategic decisions.
>
> *David Maister* (1997)

Some people argue that scenarios should only be employed to raise questions, and that they are not able to answer questions. However, the main purpose of having a view of the future is to place our business in it, and we do that because we want to achieve a prosperous future for our business. Therefore, something of the scenario has to be brought into shorter term plans as actions or at least research.

It is a myth that long-term thinking is unrelated to the struggle for next month's figures. One of the prime purposes of long-term planning is to achieve better profitability (even in the short term) through better focus.

The consumables division of a high tech company received an invitation to tender for some business which, initially, seemed very lucrative (millions of pounds). However, it did not fit in with the strategic view they had developed. So, they investigated further and decided to 'no bid', because the business would have consumed a lot of resources. It would not have been complementary to anything else they were doing and could have resulted in the company making a loss. By concentrating resources on strategic business, they improved their performance significantly and proved to themselves that the tender had indeed been diversionary. They were sure that, without having learnt to think strategically and for the long term, they would have spent a lot of resources to win that business.

However, in order to make long-term thinking relevant, we have to practise what to do with it. It is very much like rehearsing a play. A writer comes along with a script which has been accepted by the Creative Director of the theatre company and the actors read through it. Questions are asked about the writer's meaning in some passages, and some ambiguities are resolved. Then the actors start to rehearse. As they rehearse, some scenes work better than others. For those which do not work so well, variations have to be explored. When the players are happy with a particular variation, the script is amended. Rehearsals continue until everyone knows their part, and the play as a whole. Then it is an actionable proposition, ready for an audience.

The future view of the project team needs to go through a similar process of consultation with as many people as possible who are going to be involved in presenting it to the 'audience' of the business – which includes all stakeholders. It would not be sensible to do a detailed implementation plan for every variation on our most likely scenario, but we need to check that we can and should make the major themes work.

In Chapter 7 (amended by Chapter 8), we concluded that the main themes of our future scenario were:

- recognize consumer power and demand for lifestyle choices;

- recognize the specific practical needs of different age groups;

- make an opportunity out of increasing trends to shop and work from home;

- build on current strengths but meet the challenge to enter new niche markets;

- provide for corporate customers as well as consumers;

- investigate aspects of new technology which could fulfil customer needs.

These themes would result in the XYZ Furniture company of 2020 consisting of:

- XYZ Classics Division

- XYZ Logistics and recycling

- XYZ Fun Division

- XYZ Indoor/outdoor

- XYZ Nostalgia

- XYZ Senior

- XYZ Office

- XYZ Global

- XYZ Children's Division

- XYZ Furniture technology and special effects

- XYZ Furnishings consultancy

- (and XYZ Head Office)

In order to determine to what degree we can incorporate the main scenario into our shorter term plans, we need to put it through an evaluation process. This may be done by the project team or by another team – perhaps the 'murder boarding' review team. There are a number of aspects that should be examined. They are:

- strategic fit;

- product advantage;

- market opportunity;

- financial success;

- ethics;

- resource availability.

The framework of evaluation criteria discussed here is based on that used in a software prototype developed by Steve Cook, formerly a PhD student at Cranfield.

'First pass' evaluation of the main scenario

Strategic fit

The aspect of success which tops the list in product concept evaluation is establishing that the product is in line with the corporate image and mission. Unless your company has set out to be a conglomerate, diversification is widely considered to be the highest risk strategic option. Because of this acknowledged risk, trouble shooter Sir John Harvey Jones frequently advises companies featured on his television programmes to 'stick to their knitting'.

'Sticking to your knitting' does not mean stagnation. If an organization's mission is to fulfil identifiable customer needs, innovation can still be dramatic. In the nineteenth century, the railway was a revolution in travel. Railway companies were hugely successful. However, in the twentieth century, railway companies stuck to running railways and went into decline. Had they seen their mission as fulfilling people's need to get from A to B, they might have developed buses and cars as well.

We discussed mission in Chapter 4. A company's mission should always be flexible enough to accommodate dramatic change if that dramatic change is complementary to the firm's historical development. 3M originally fulfilled the need for polishing surfaces by producing sandpaper, they developed products for doing other things with surfaces, such as adhesives and reflective materials, they diversified more widely as well, but they are still leading the world in abrasives technology. XYZ Furniture company fulfils customer needs for function, comfort and aesthetics in the home. Our main scenario for the company is consistent with that mission. It even ensures that it is carried to new horizons by addressing new niche markets.

In addition to this 'high level' fit with mission, we need to check the effect of the scenario on existing strategies.

Products/services

Product/service strategy should not be about technological capabilities, but it should establish the company's approach to product development. Is the company an innovator, willing to set targets such as '40 per cent of our sales must always come from products which are less than five years old'? Is the company an incremental developer, continuously improving tried and tested formulae? Is the company a follower of others?

XYZ has never set out to follow or copy any other company, nor has it been a fashion leader. Raising XYZ to the role of innovator would require considerable investment and culture change. Tactical acquisitions of niche innovators might be required to 'kick-start' the transformation.

Processes

Process excellence is not optional, it is a prerequisite strategy for every company that intends to be around for a long time. In fact, 'reducing hassle factors' is the most important thing a supplier can do to win and keep customers. If your company is extremely difficult to deal with, that 'pit of the stomach' bad feeling, which customers experience when they are trying to check an invoice and have been put on hold for the third time, will send you out of business sooner rather than later.

No supplier has an automatic right to customers' business, and it takes concentrated effort to make it so easy to deal with your company that customers would not bother to try anywhere else. Building up 'exit barriers' are worth that effort.

In the case of relationships with retailers, there should be smooth, consistent interfaces at every transaction level and function between the organizations. Top management commitment will be demonstrated by meetings to discuss strategy with the retailer. Information flow should be streamlined, and information systems integration will be planned or in place. Transaction costs will be reduced and time will be taken out of work cycles.

The equivalent has to be achieved for end customers also. If they telephone the company's Help Line, they should be able to get through immediately to someone who can give them good advice about everything from mending a cupboard door that their 4 year old has used as a swing, to getting an egg stain out of a cream velvet cushion cover. Any paperwork between the customer and XYZ should be handled efficiently and accurately. They should be introduced to top managers via newsletters and therefore know who they are if they want to make a complaint.

The main scenario requires a special effort in terms of process excellence. Whilst XYZ has never been the worst in the business for process quality, it has never been the best either. Offering the end-customer the opportunity to shop from home requires new processes, which must be as simple as possible. Entering new niche markets means that more choice is provided and therefore much more expertise must be available to customers. Project by project, and utilizing new information systems and process skills, XYZ will have to invest.

Place/channels

Place is part of the customer experience, but it is increasingly flexible. Twenty years ago, furniture brands had to be in retail outlets, and customers would judge a brand by what sort of outlets stocked it, and how accessible they were. Today, channels to market include a greater variety of retail options, and direct routes via catalogues, television shopping and the Internet. In 20 years' time, there might be even more. XYZ has a number of decisions to make about the future make-up of its location and channel possibilities:

- where to locate manufacturing capability;

- where to locate stockholding for bought-in items;

- how to transport physical goods around markets;

- what channels to use.

The scenario for XYZ does require the incorporation of new 'place' and 'channel' options into company strategy. The hidden challenge is the development of relationships with intermediaries in the market map and directly with customers, and the management of all the information that will be needed to drive communications and delivery of physical goods in a 'no hassle' way. XYZ may have to recruit or develop new expertise to manage 'place' and 'channel' strategy. Alternatively, the company may acquire skills from the proposed joint venture with leading charities, many of whom have excellent experience in logistics, which is a key factor in dealing with international crises.

Promotion

The payback from promotional activity is becoming easier to measure. The important thing is to choose a consistent message and a consistent method which is most appropriate to each product group and then to use both consistently. The promotional portfolio of XYZ in 20 years' time might look like that set out in Table 9.1.

Once again, the most likely scenario is leading XYZ into promotional techniques it has never before explored. Additional expertise will be required, both from specialist agencies and within the company.

People

Persistent publicity for the 'stakeholder society' has persuaded many companies that they want to be 'Investors In People'. Those companies that are endeavouring very hard to invest in their employees are reaping worthwhile rewards. A manufacturing company in Brazil called Semco has become one of South America's fastest growing companies after empowering all employees to take decisions previously made by

TABLE 9.1   XYZ's portfolio for 20 years' time

Product Group	Message	Method
XYZ Classics Division	Reliability and style	■ Joint promotions with retailers – local media ■ Loyalty scheme ■ Encourage personal recommendations via incentives
XYZ Logistics and recycling	XYZ commitment to the environment	Press and public relations
XYZ Fun Division	Novelty	Direct contact with target customers (e.g. parents of teenage children)
XYZ Indoor/outdoor	Versatility	Lifestyle magazines
XYZ Nostalgia	Recreating a great atmosphere	Direct contact with target customers (by age of purchaser, or age of their home)
XYZ Office	Practicality and comfort	Magazines and newspapers read by business professionals
XYZ Global	Recreating an alternative view of home comfort	Selective joint promotions, e.g. Japanese theme with Japanese restaurant
XYZ Children's Division	Fun and durability	Joint promotions with specialist shops for children
XYZ Furniture technology and special effects	XYZ at the cutting edge	Press and public relations
XYZ Furnishings consultancy	Create something totally individual and special	Trade press (hotels, offices) Top style magazines (individuals) plus face-to-face selling

managers. (Managers are not redundant, they just do more important things than they did before.)

Meanwhile, other companies make the right noises, but fail to follow through. In *The Dilbert Principle*, Scott Adams (1996) names 'Employees are our most valuable asset' as the first Great Lie of Management, which is how it seems to many employees in companies which lack commitment to them.

XYZ has to decide whether it is going to be a hierarchy or a democracy. Has the company been built on military discipline or open communication? To date, XYZ has hardly had a 'people' strategy. It has been a relatively paternalistic firm, it has overcome its problems with the trade unions, and is neither a particularly good nor a particularly bad employer.

Dramatic change will certainly require employee goodwill. It will also require a great deal of communication. Semco found initially that workers felt that they hated bosses and did not want to talk to them, until they discovered that talking to bosses got results. (Bosses also discovered that talking to workers got them results too.) Now there is a waiting list of thousands of Brazilians hoping to work for the company.

It is difficult to imagine the individualistic consumers we have painted in our future view going to work and tolerating any degree of totalitarianism. A lot of successful firms will be creative teams of responsible adults producing quality products that people want in the best possible working environment. It will not be the only formula, but it is a particularly fond dream of many entrepreneurs still deeply involved in their companies that people should really, *really want* to work for them. They can envisage the power of a highly motivated workforce. Bureaucratic organizations where ownership is diffuse or embodied in something intangible such as 'the public purse' might find it more difficult to make the changes necessary to achieve such competitive advantage.

The XYZ+20 team's main scenario presents the human resources manager with the challenge of facilitating communications and motivation to much higher levels than the company currently enjoys.

Price

'Cost plus' pricing has been hammered by successive recessions and the emergence of vast amounts of choice for industrial and consumer buying decision makers. In many industry to industry sales, open book negotiations and 'value pricing' have ensured that customers more or less decide what they are prepared to pay to keep their supplier in business. After decades of adversarial haggling over price, which sometimes resulted in customers insisting on unprofitable deals, some British companies supplying Japanese entrants into the UK car market in the 1980s found their willingness to let them make a profit amazingly refreshing.

Can we imagine, in 20 years' time, that companies might be required to deliver goods at cost to consumers and then ask for a 'tip' according to how much they enjoy the product? Also, prices may have to change daily or even hourly, according to offers traded on the Internet. The home computer may enable electronic trading in all sorts of consumer goods, so that something like a share index is developed.

In the meantime, the XYZ sales and marketing department has to make careful judgements about the challenges of generating volume and profit. Market leaders tend to be the most profitable players in their industry, but they have to have established volume (and thus share) first. The project team has precluded the use of discounts and trivial short-term tactics in the main scenario. So careful research of loyalty-based promotional techniques and brand-building advertising will be required.

Financing the business and the structure of capital and ownership

One of the starkest inhibitors of growth is the ability of the company to fund it. JCB has managed 'organic' growth, through reinvestment of profits, to take it from a one-man enterprise to a global company in 50 years. It is one of the few global companies which is still owned privately by one family. In most companies, especially those in fast moving industries, the entrepreneur has had to dilute capital by seeking support from venture capitalists or business angels. The alternative is to borrow from financial institutions, regarded by most who own their own businesses as high risk due to the short-term payback usually expected. Since XYZ has a 20 year outlook on its ambitions, high risk financing can be minimized.

XYZ is a family owned company (with some employee shareholding), and cash rich enough for pump-priming some degree of investment, which will kick-start the plan. However, the 2020 view will require an open-minded approach to funding expansion in the future, and some tactical borrowing from banks may be necessary. In addition, the concept of wider share ownership is implied in the scenario: for employees, as compensation for acquired businesses, as an aspect of partnership with certain suppliers or customers, etc.

In concluding this discussion of strategic fit, which is most important to the successful implementation of any aspects of the XYZ+20 team's scenario, we note that the scenario does not actually clash with current strategy, but that it is an indication of the weakness of current strategy. Fulfilling the main scenario certainly presents some challenges to almost every aspect of the business. The example illustrates why foundations have to be built now to achieve the long-term vision of the company. Further evaluation topics need to be explored as well.

Product advantage

Will our main scenario ensure that in 20 years time or before, we are offering the customer enough:

- product superiority;

- product quality;

- unique benefits;

- problem-solving;

- use of advanced technology;

to ensure that they choose us before all others?

Common sense dictates that if the advantages of the new XYZ are merely superficial, customers may well stick to the established solution. Many companies are 'me-too' or provide a difference of no relevance to the customer, but five out of seven major components of market impact are associated with product advantage. It is the dominant factor in success.

This emphasis on product advantage does not preclude continuous improvement. The first drill manufacturer to provide the same drills as last year but with longer leads and integral plugs was meeting four out of five of these criteria – apparently minor changes can deliver dramatic improvements in superiority, quality, uniqueness and problem-solving.

In the case of the XYZ+20 project team's main scenario:

- product superiority is through design;

- product quality has to be continuously improved;

- unique benefits are associated with design and choice;

- the degree of problem-solving is not clear in a product sense, but we may be able to make it easier for the customer to do business with XYZ rather than competitors;

- the use of advanced technology may not be apparent in the manufacturing of furniture, but in the management of information about customers and communications with customers.

The degree of product advantage which we can derive from the scenario may not seem to be sufficient. For this reason, a project for the shorter term plan would be to explore the pursuit of product advantage in more detail. The output from that might require the furniture technology division to be set up sooner rather than later, not to mention encouraging ideas from everyone in the company.

In addition, the project team must take into account elements of risk associated with new product portfolios, and make sure that they are avoided:

- *The product proves to be inadequate.* The most common cause of inadequacy is likely to be that the product or service is not of a high enough quality, or sufficiently different from what it replaces, to meet customer expectations. I have heard senior managers (who ought to know better) declare that marketing can compensate for a weak product. It can't.

- *The product proves to be too complex.* The most common cause of quality problems is over-complexity. Especially when a product is introduced, it ought not to need lots of bells and whistles. It ought to have one overridingly clear advantage over what has gone before. Even with services, such as savings accounts, customers can be confused by too many features, and consequently be hesitant. Meanwhile there is money being wasted in the administration of these features.

A creative approach to minimizing product risks is to share them with companies who have a mutual strategic interest in the outcome. Can XYZ identify any potential partners in their future scenario? Suppliers and retailers are possible candidates, design companies would be desirable, but even competitors should be considered. Joint ventures in certain markets could be mutually beneficial.

Market opportunity

Closely related to product advantage is the nature of the market opportunity which XYZ will be able to realize if the main scenario is fulfilled. Minor product changes provide only short windows of market opportunity, as it is easy for competitors to follow.

Products which fulfil vague needs can command a significant lead, but they require an extensive amount of promotional spend to realize their market opportunity. A great many packs of Post-it notes were given away before they commanded the premium price they hold today. Canderel commands a high price because of its product advantages over other sweeteners and sugar, but it was still many years before product development costs were recouped. It still has to be heavily advertised on television. Fashionable young people were paid to walk around Tokyo with Sony Walkmans when they were first developed, in order to arouse interest in a product for which there was no apparent market!

XYZ, to be market leader, must obviously achieve a dominant market share. The underlying assumption of our most likely scenario is that XYZ should have a significant market share in the whole of the furniture market in the UK by 2020, and be doing much more business in export markets. It sounds daunting for an 'also-ran' only operating in the UK at the moment. XYZ have 20 years to achieve it, but decisions have to be made now about the first steps towards it.

Growth in the market is another factor of market opportunity. The population size of north west Europe is, on average, stable. Identifying pockets of above average growth, such as the large number of young people in the Republic of Ireland, is the relevant challenge in making market share inroads.

Last, but not least, time is a factor of market opportunity. Many marvellous new concepts have been launched on to the market and taken much longer than expected to be adopted by consumers. It is important for XYZ to plot its expansion over a long period of time.

Market opportunity also has to be balanced with market risks, such as:

- *Cannibalizing existing products*. Will the creation of new markets mean that existing ones shrink in size? Undoubtedly, the answer is 'yes'. It is a lot safer if the company is operating in both, rather than putting all its eggs into one or the other.

- *Customer mismanagement of the product/service*. Customer service experts now suggest that good service means not just putting right your own mistakes, but those that the customer might make as well.

- *Being late to market*. Can you be sure you are going to be first?

- *Customer loyalty*. Is the customer group you want to buy your new product actively discontented with what they have at the moment? Customer loyalty is not necessarily a reason for failing to initiate change, but it does affect the size of the accessible market for a new product.

Financial success

The most likely scenario demands considerable investment from XYZ's family owners. Most previous investments have been made on the basis of payback over 5 years which would be greater than leaving the money in the money markets. In asking whether or not our scenario leads us towards a much more profitable future, we must also look critically at the payback period, remembering that JCB waited 13 years for profit from their entry into the US market. If XYZ is truly becoming a future-oriented company, the discounted cash flow for the whole of XYZ+20 ought to be phased over 25 years.

After project planning, it will be possible to progress XYZ+20 module by module. Comparisons can then be made between initiatives, and a balance may emerge between quick payback projects and those which offer longer term advantages. At this stage we can only make deductions based on the known advantages enjoyed by the current market leader compared to XYZ's current profitability. The indications are that investment is necessary to avoid future disadvantage as well as to gain advantage in the longer term (Figure 9.1).

Lack of investment would result in a company going out of business within 5 years. The results of investing ought to provide an acceptable

FIGURE 9.1   Gap analysis – XYZ Furniture and a competitior

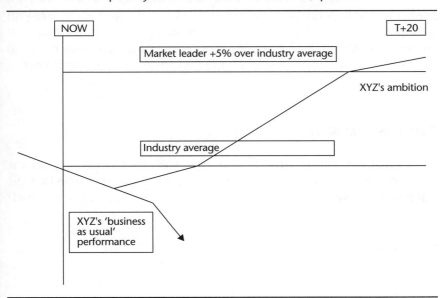

return within 5 years. Returns would accelerate with the advantages of gaining market share.

Ethics

Companies do not have to be Ben and Jerry's, the Co-operative Bank or Body Shop to be affected by ethical issues. Almost every day there is media coverage of high profile court cases involving poor ethics, or at least a lack of care, in business. Mis-selling of pensions, illegal share dealing, addictive pharmaceuticals, faulty car design, dangerous toys, holidays in unbuilt hotels and food unfit for human consumption are all familiar themes.

The general rule these days, is that business ethics and environmental considerations should be both strategic imperatives and consistent daily concerns. The challenge is not just to avoid being unethical or making mistakes which could harm customers, it is to make positive progress through concentration on moral and considerate business behaviour.

The XYZ+20 team has devoted considerable thought to safety, quality and environmental issues. It does assume that the company will take the recycling of furniture very seriously, that it will research environmental improvements for all styles, and there is the potential for the technology division to experiment with special functions for special needs. In addition the company would probably wish to establish a simple code of conduct for employees about openness in dealings with all fellow stakeholders and keeping promises to them. Thereafter, XYZ as a whole will be more widely admired by customers and prospective customers.

Resource availability

The availability and synergy of resources is another vital angle on the implementation of aspects of a scenario for 2020. Consider whether the following are likely to be available when and where they will be required?

- funds;

- people;

- skills;

- physical space;

- appropriate equipment;

- information;

- information system support;

A *force field*, as illlustrated in Figure 9.2, will be particularly helpful in addressing resource issues:

The horizontal line in Figure 9.2 represents equilibrium, or neutrality. Each vertical line north of the horizontal line represents a 'help' factor. The length of the line indicates the degree of help – the longer the line, the more favourable the situation. Each vertical line south of the horizontal line represents a 'hindrance' factor. The length of the line indicates the degree of hindrance – the longer the line, the more unfavourable the situation.

Good programmes and projects can fail because of resource constraints. In this example, there are some very positive 'help' factors, but big 'hindrance' factors as well. By exploring problems in advance,

FIGURE 9.2   Force field analysis

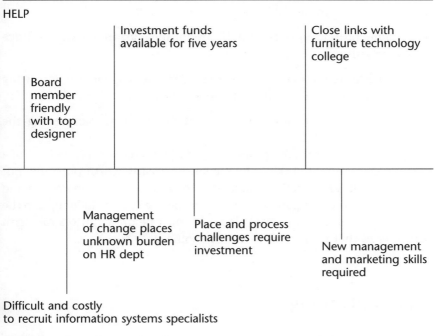

HELP

Investment funds available for five years

Close links with furniture technology college

Board member friendly with top designer

Management of change places unknown burden on HR dept

Place and process challenges require investment

New management and marketing skills required

Difficult and costly to recruit information systems specialists

HINDRANCE

solutions can be found and/or contingencies arranged. Project managers get an immense feeling of satisfaction when circumstances throw a spanner into the works and they have already got 'Plan B' ready and waiting in their drawer. Others believe that it is only when there is a Plan B in the drawer that any project has any hope of going according to plan.

Before we consider project planning, the evaluation team can summarize the effect of the scenario on XYZ's strategic positioning:

- Product innovation needs more concentration in order to establish greater product advantage.

- Process excellence will also be prerequisite.

- New channels to market must be developed.

- New promotional messages and methods will also be required.

- Environmental and ethical considerations (such as safety) need more attention.

- Greater involvement of the workforce will facilitate the degree of change envisaged.

- Investment in new skills will be considerable.

- Value propositions should be established as the basis for price comparisons.

- Organic growth may need to be supplemented by tactical borrowing if all market opportunities are to be explored.

The team should measure the degree of fit of the scenario using the categories in Table 9.2.

The total score for the proposed scenario is a respectable 755 out of a possible maximum of 1,000. The scenario is clearly worth pursuing, but there are still some major challenges to overcome. In order to build confidence in the company's ability to tackle the bigger challenges in the longer term, some 'easy to do' elements must be drawn into short-term planning so that project teams can see some early successes.

Project planning

Planning can put individuals in control of their work and companies in control of markets. Research from a variety of sources indicates that

TABLE 9.2   Summary checklist

Factor	weight	score	weight × score
Strategic fit	15	5	75
Product advantage	10	7	70
Market opportunity	20	9	180
Financial success	30	9	270
Ethics	10	10	100
Resource availability	15	4	60
TOTAL	100		755

Weightings are a percentage
10 = highest, 1 = lowest

planning and contingency planning makes a positive contribution to company performance, and to employee performance, especially when 'why' is as prominent as 'how' in the distributed plan. But, the more items, activities and interdependencies there are in the project plan, the higher the risk of implementation problems.

Professional project managers are now equipped with sophisticated software to create project plans. They can define individual tasks in the project and their interdependencies to produce an optimum route to completion, or a number of suitable alternatives using the Programme Evaluation and Review Technique (PERT). For the manager who is not a project management professional but has to make sure that things get done, a GANTT chart which plots progress over time, and action plans for individuals, are often used.

In the case of XYZ+20, the potential complexity of project planning makes it essential to break down the scenario into smaller projects which can in turn be broken down into tasks to be managed, as illustrated in Figure 9.3.

In this case shown in Figure 9.3, the XYZ+20 scenario would be defined as *the programme*. Although we may think that we have defined it in as much detail as is relevant at this stage, if we are going to make any of it work, it needs to be thought through to a much finer degree of detail.

The project team must work out how to achieve the programme by treating it as a business game with 20 rounds. What has to be done in each year to achieve market leadership at the end of the game must be worked out. In addition, the murder boarding team, and perhaps another team, should be brought in to play the game, in order to establish alternative routes. A sponsoring senior manager should introduce

FIGURE 9.3 Management by projects. Adapted from Ralph Levene, Cranfield School of Management

Strategic direction through management by projects

Programme				
Project	Project	Project	Project	Project
Tasks				

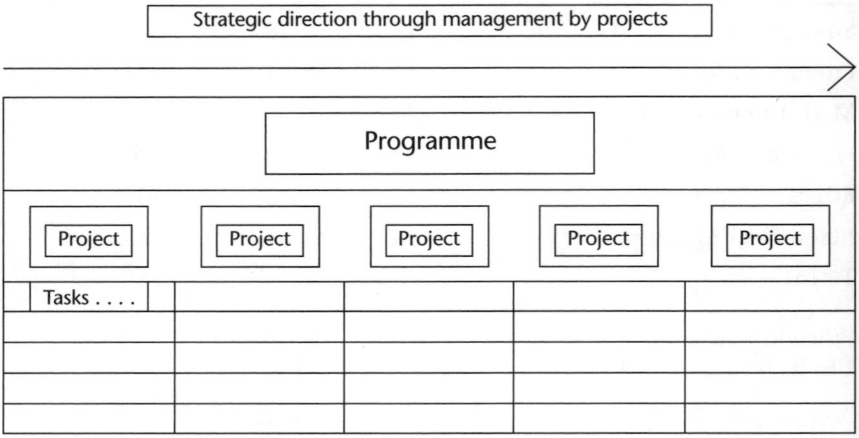

periodic hazards, to see how the team copes with a competitor's attempts to thwart XYZ's progress.

Most of the first 'virtual' three months of the business game will be spent on project planning. The massive change described in the scenario has to be broken down, stage by stage, as is demonstrated in Figure 9.4.

The teams also have to consider the fact that the planning cycle will have to be reiterated several times over the 'virtual' 20 years. However, for the first few rounds, their decisions will be guided by use of a matrix as shown in Figure 9.5 – slightly modified from that used in the last chapter.

FIGURE 9.4 Project planning stage by stage. From Levene, Cranfield School of Management

Strategy formulation	Programme Assembly	Project definition and identification of tasks	Project implementation	Monitoring and control

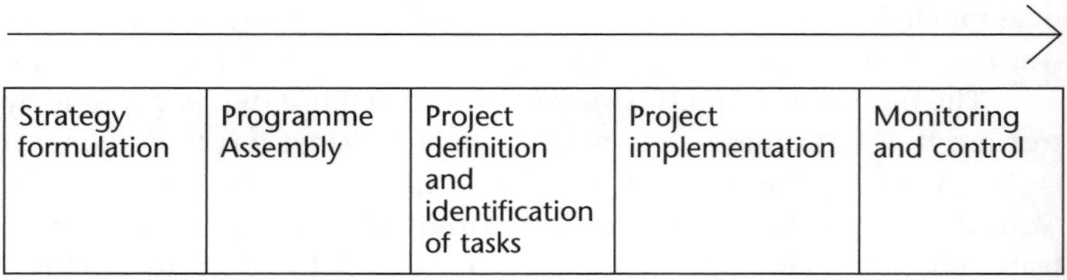

FIGURE 9.5   Ease of implementation matrix. From Cole (1996)

Ease of implementation

	Easy	Difficult
High	*Quick hits*	*Strategic wins?*
Impact on customer choice	*Infrastructure building*	
Low		

We assume that no team will pursue activities which are difficult to do and have a low impact on customer choice.

In the case of XYZ+20, the picture in Figure 9.6 might emerge from one or more of the teams' deliberations in the first stage of the game.

The XYZ+20 project has been broken down into modules, which can be treated as separate projects. Since the company is in decline, it is desirable to tackle the expansion activities the teams regard as lower risk first of all, whilst building an infrastructure which is going to underpin the prosperous future of the company. Priorities might emerge as listed in Table 9.3.

FIGURE 9.6 Ease of implementation matrix from the first stage. From Cole (1996).

	Ease of implementation	
	Easy (1–5 years)	Difficult (5+ years)
High	*Quick hits* ■ Consultancy (trade) ■ Office ■ Indoor/outdoor	*Strategic wins* ■ Lifestyle divisions ■ Process excellence
Impact on customer choice	*Infrastructure building* ■ Establish technology centre ■ Recycling scheme ■ Product quality ■ Internet activity	
Low		

Year 5 can be ear-marked for consolidation and review activities. The first five rounds of the business game may look like Table 9.4.

Each team has managed to considerably improve the position of XYZ over 5 years. Arguably, Team 3 have achieved the best position because the greater increase in sales must mean a better market share which will provide more sustainable profit growth than Team 2, who have been somewhat more risk-averse in their approach. Team 1 over-stretched the company's resources and ability to change in Year 1, and failed to recover enough to be responsive as well as pro-active.

TABLE 9.3 XYZ's project priorities

Timing	Priority (per year)	Project
Y1, Q2–on-going	1	Process excellence
On-going	1a	Internet activity
Y1, Q3–Y2, Q3	2, 2	Establish or acquire office range (trade and consumers)
Y1, Q1–Y1, Q3	3	Establish consultancy service for big trade customers
Y1, Q4–every year	4	Product quality, safety, etc.
Y2, Q1–Y2, Q3	1	Establish or acquire indoor/outdoor range
Y2, Q2–on-going	3	Establishment of recycling scheme with appropriate charities, public bodies
Y3	1	Establish technology centre
Y4	1	Incorporate better environmental materials, etc.

At this point, the teams may stop and draw breath, and consider what has been learnt so far. And then consider the following:

Suppose if you invent a good guess, calculate the consequences and discover that they all agree with experiments. The theory is then right? No, it is simply not proved wrong, because in the future there could be a wider range of experiments, you compute a wider range of consequences and you may then discover that the theory is wrong.
Richard Feynman, Nobel prize winning physicist, 1964 Cornell lecture

The project team had developed a future scenario, and tested it to destruction. They knew why they believe it is worth planning for it. As Feynman went on to explain – even in something as logical as physics, 'laws' sometimes keep working until all of a sudden something else comes along and shows that they are at worst wrong and at best incomplete. The circumstances thrown in at random by the sponsor of the business game show how some plausible external impacts, especially competitor activity, may force adaptation of the business' chosen path.

Realized strategy will be a combination of developed strategy and emergent strategy. The accommodation of emergent strategy into

TABLE 9.4 The first five rounds of the business game

Year	Environment set by sponsor	Team activity	Cumulative results
1	Modest economic growth	Team 1 Process excellence (+Internet) Establish office range Establish consultancy Start quality initiative	Sales +10% Profit −15%
	Competitors complacent	Team 2 Start quality initiative Establish office range Establish indoor/outdoor	Sales +20% Profit −20%
	Social trends moving forward as forecast in XYZ+20	Team 3 Recycling scheme Establish office range Process excellence (+Internet)	Sales +10% Profit −10%
2	Mild recession Government concerns about furniture safety for the elderly	Team 1 Establish indoor/outdoor collection Continue work on office range Set up recycling scheme	Sales +30% Profit −05%
	Competitor introduces special effects furniture	Team 2 Process excellence Consultancy for trade customers	Sales +40% Profit 00%
	Social trends moving forward as forecast in XYZ+20	Team 3 Quality initiatives Set up technology centre Establish XYZ Seniors	Sales +35% Profit +01%
3	Economic boom European Directive banning foam as furniture component	Team 1 Establish technology centre	Sales +35% Profit -05%
	Major competitors merge	Team 2 Take advantage of economic boom with 'Classics'	Sales +45% Profit +10%
	Sociologists report increasing conservatism in tastes of baby boomers as they reach retirement age	Team 3 Be first to market with foam replacement Establish indoor/outdoor	Sales +65% Profit +10%

Year	Environment set by sponsor	Team activity	Cumulative results
4	Modest economic growth	Team 1 Be first to market with foam replacement Test market XYZ Nostalgia prototypes via Internet	Sales +55% Profit +05%
	Competitors launch lifestyle catalogue	Team 2 Get closer to retailers Establish technology centre	Sales +50% Profit +20%
	Popular TV drama creates craze for 1960s styles	Team 3 Consultancy for trade customers Launch lifestyle catalogue Pilot Nostalgia range (1960s) in TV magazines	Sales +65% Profit +15%
5	Economic stagnation Government raises extra taxes on luxury goods	Team 1 Lower prices Launch loyalty scheme for Classics Build customer databases	Sales +60% Profit +10%
	Niche lifestyle competitor goes bust Merged competitor recognized as market leader in UK	Team 2 Lower prices on Classics Improve processes Improve Internet presence Launch lifestyle mail order	Sales +55% Profit +18%
	The generation brought up on home computers comes of age and shuns shopping	Team 3 Improve value offer on Classics Expand Internet activity Buy lifestyle furniture company (market entrant)	Sales +75% Profit +16%

developed strategy shows an ability to adapt, innovate and learn. That is why Team 3's approach seems to be the most attractive. Team 3 have also been prepared to take risks.

> Boldness, directed by an overruling intelligence, is the stamp of the hero: this boldness does not consist in venturing directly against the nature of things, . . . The more boldness lends wings to the mind and the discernment, so much the farther they will reach in their flight . . . but certainly always only in the sense that with greater objects, greater dangers are connected.
>
> *Carl von Clausewitz. Prussian General*

The whole point of making a plan is to establish a basis for measuring progress. But it is not a Stalinist plan which must be implemented, or appear to be implemented, regardless of changing realities. It is a basis for analysis and learning. If something changes, revisit the plan. Even if something on which you based the plan changes significantly, re-iterate the thinking process to find the solution and hone your planning skills. Planning is not useless because something did not work out – every time that happens, we learn something for the next plan. We have to adjust and move on – keeping our planning philosophy in mind even if the precise performance does not always fit.

If success does not come quickly enough, and playing the business game is a way of gauging what can be achieved in what timescale, adjustments have to be made.

> All you can tell people is to keep their eyes open, embrace ambiguity, and don't be frightened of surprise.
>
> *Warren Bennis, industrial psychologist*

The game could continue for another fifteen rounds, or another three teams might be assembled to try the first 5 years again, until the sponsor is confident that a truly inspired plan has been devised.

Task planning

Once the appropriate format of projects which will kick off the XYZ+20 programme have been identified, those projects will subsequently have to be broken down into tasks. Table 9.5 illustrates this process for the project to establish a recycling scheme.

TABLE 9.5 Project breakdown – establishing a recycling scheme

Action	Who leads?	Who else involved?	Deadline	Resource implication
Contact all charities and public bodies who might be able to use second hand furniture	Managing Director's PA	MD	T+ 8 weeks	5 person days: research letters telephone calls
Shortlist three to five organizations with most frequent need	Managing Director's PA	MD	T+ 12 weeks	5 person days: research discussions
Research possible logistical system	Logistics Manager	Charities Other transport and technical staff	T + 20 weeks	15 person days Research Site visits Meetings
Pilot possible logistical system for three months	Logistics Manager	Charities Drivers who volunteer for pilot	T + 32 weeks	Time and cost impact will be an outcome of the pilot
Decision on preferred methodology	Managing Director	Charities Logistics	T + 36 weeks	3 person days preparing report
Launch scheme	Managing Director	Charities Logistics Marketing	T + 40 weeks	Time and costs involved in press and public relations

Impact on customer: Low
Ease of implementation: High

In effect, it all boils down to a list of things to do. However, the doing comes after the thinking. As we discussed in Chapter 1, Hamel and Prahalad (1994) found that managers spend (on average) less than 3 per cent of their time building a corporate perspective on the future. They suggest that best practice would be 20–50 per cent. Without the thinking about the future, what those managers do from day-to-day could be totally futile.

If we have an ineffective strategy and pursue it with alacrity we will only hasten our organization's demise. Once we have an effective strategic framework, such as the XYZ+20 scenario, and have explored how it might affect the regular activity of the business, working out the efficient way to implement it is straightforward (Figure 9.7).

FIGURE 9.7   Strategy diagram. Adapted from McDonald (1984).

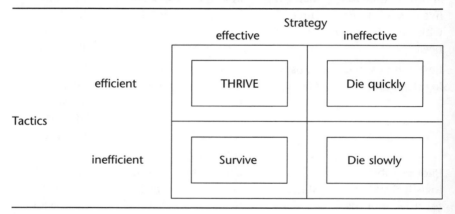

Monitoring

In order to keep both strategy and implementation on track, every item in the planning framework needs to be regularly reviewed and re-iterated. The following schedule shown in Figure 9.8 is generally applied.

In addition, an unusual or dramatic event should prompt an *ad hoc* check of its effect on the plans.

The purpose of monitoring is not just to make sure that plans are adjusted in the light of especially favourable or unfavourable external impacts, but also to ensure that adjustments are not counter-strategic. If XYZ has a value-pricing strategy, then it is most definitely not a discounter. Therefore Team 2's price-cutting reaction to an economic recession would have caused concern. If XYZ wants to be at the forefront of new developments in the furniture industry, its plans for a technology centre

FIGURE 9.8   Review schedule

Long range Corporate Outlook 20–30 years		Annual reviews 3-yearly re-iteration
Strategic Business and Marketing Plan 3–5 years	Quarterly reviews Annual re-iteration	
Segment Plans Account Plans		
One year action plan	Monthly reviews Annual re-iteration	

should not be shelved at the first sign of adversity. Adjustment, to a public–private partnership with the best furniture technology college in Europe might be acceptable, if such a deal were on offer. Judgements are often difficult, because implementing strategy is much more difficult than devising it. However, a strategic framework makes decision-making considerably easier than shooting in the dark. It is not how much people do for XYZ which will make the company succeed, it is doing the right things.

SUMMARY:

In this chapter we have:
- evaluated the most likely scenario for its effect on:
  - strategic fit;
  - product advantage;
  - market opportunity;
  - financial success;
  - ethics;
  - resource availability;
- practised project planning via a business simulation game;
- reviewed task planning;
- considered on-going monitoring of the strategic framework provided by the scenario.

Conclusion

The nicest thing about not planning is that failure comes as a complete surprise, and is not preceded by a period of worry and depression.

John Perton, Boston College

We all love hindsight. It is a wonderful thing. Looking back and thinking – if only we had thought of that or done that. When we do, it is surprising how many times we think that we ought to have seen the event coming. The clues to the future are in the past. We need to notice what is staring us in the face, add a bit of imagination to carry it to its logical conclusion, and we can have hindsight in advance. It is called foresight. If we go for this approach, then actual hindsight is more likely to be congratulatory than full of regret.

European companies surveyed by Gill Ringland (1997) reported that scenario planning leads to more flexible short-term planning, improved cross-company teamwork and shared corporate values, a heightened awareness of the opportunities and threats inherent in the changing business environment and an enhanced ability to accommodate that change. It also leads to greater confidence in the strategic solutions the company chooses to follow.

From my own experience, the main benefit for companies large and small to whom I have introduced this technique is that it instils a greater sense of urgency about change, but change in the context of the time continuum. In other words, businesses need to embrace a future which accommodates and learns from the past.

Coca-Cola spent $2 million on 200,000 taste tests on a new recipe for their world-beating cola. The results were that the vast majority of tasters liked the new Coke better than the original. A few said that they would like the choice of both. Only these few respondents had tried to relate their attitude of preferring new Coke, to their likely behaviour – wanting both.

Coca-Cola overlooked that feedback, and when they launched New Coke they *withdrew* Old Coke. This created uproar, and the whole thing descended into fiasco. They failed to accommodate the past with the future.

The thinking process recommended in this book has relevance to decision makers in all organizations, product based and service based, public and private, for this very obvious reason:

> Without rising revenues, companies will find it steadily harder to offer shareholders and staff the rewards they seek. . .
>
> *Peter Martin*

Those rising revenues have to be imagined, and where they come from.

The benefits of ensuring that long-term, speculative and imaginative thinking takes place are many. This process develops the thinking skills of the participants, and their ability to cope with risk and uncertainty. They will become more effective observers of the business environment. Appreciating the uncertain will facilitate more creativity in the relationship between strategy and tactics, and leads to better short-term decision-making. Participants practise identifying opportunities for competitive edge, and will carry that through to their day-to-day activities. They will also be prepared for difficult business circumstances, and be prepared to devise solutions well in advance. They will make sure that they have time to think, so that they may at least mould the company for change, and at best seize advantage from the future. They will demonstrate increased confidence through involvement in strategy. Their thinking skills will feed directly into innovation of all kinds.

The beauty of this is, it is low risk! Although the time involved costs money, there is not a lot to lose, and it will be time well spent in team building and developing managerial skills as well as identifying winning strategies. Varying levels of risk are of course associated with plan implementation, and should be identified. There are plenty of examples of failing to prepare for the future leading to disaster. Ask company doctors about the main cause of company failure, and they will put ignoring changing business environments, markets and competitive situations at the top of the list. So, in the spirit of learning from the mistakes of the past, practise and enjoy seizing the future for your organization, before it is too late!

Bibliography

Adams, Scott (1996) *The Dilbert Principle*, New York, Harper Collins.

Arkin, Anat (1997) 'The secret of his success', *People Management*, 23 October.

Barwise, Patrick (1995) 'Strategic investment decisions and emergent strategy', 'Mastering Management' series in the *Financial Times*.

Bauer, E. E. (1990) *Boeing in Peace and War*, Seattle, Taba Publishing.

Bell, Blackler and Crump (1997) 'Look smart', *People Management*, 23 October.

Boulton, Leyla (1997) 'BP to lift sales of solar equipment to $1bn', *Financial Times*, 17/18 May.

Business Consulting (1997) 'Planning for uncertainty', November.

Carnegy, Hugh (1995) 'Scared of growing fat and lazy', *Financial Times*, 10 July.

von Clausewitz, Carl (1832) *On War*.

Cole, Andy (1996) 'Realising the benefits of change', *Project Manager Today*, October.

Coles, Margaret (1997) 'Managing the culture shock', *Sunday Times*, 23 March.

Collins, James, and Porras, Jerry (1995) 'How the best stay at the top', *Director*, June.

Cookson, Clive (1997) 'Real innovation meets hostility', *Financial Times*, 12 September.

Day, George, and Reibstein, David (1995) 'Keeping ahead in the competitive game', 'Mastering Management' series in the *Financial Times*.

Davidson, Hugh (1997) *Even More Offensive Marketing*, Penguin, London.

Director (1997) 'In conversation with Warren Bennis', September.

Director (1997) 'Booming conservatives', November.

Feynman, Richard (1964) Cornell Lecture.

Hamel, Gary and Prahalad, C. K. (1994) *Competing for the Future*, Boston, Harvard Business School Press.

Hamel, Gary and Prahalad, C. K. (1995) 'Are you creating tomorrow's markets?', *Director*, January.

Handy, Charles (1997) 'A future of service with a smile', *Management Today*, March.

Handy, Charles (1997) 'A hard act for business to follow, *Management Today*, July.

Harrison, Tracey (1997) 'Dust the job', *Daily Mirror*, 1 December.

Hecht, Françoise (1997) 'The gold diggers', *Director*, May.

Huthwaite Researched Effectiveness, (1997) 'Why change initiatives fail'.

Janis, Irving (1971) 'Groupthink', *Psychology Today*, November.

Kakabadse, Ludlow and Vinnicombe (1988) *Working in Organisations*, London, Penguin Business.

Kennedy, Carol (1997) '50 and still nifty', *Director*, October.

Kennedy, Carol (1997) 'From competing to value innovation', *MBA*, December.

Kotler, Philip (1991) *Marketing Management*, Prentice-Hall.

Levene, Ralph (1997) 'Project Management is Business Management', *Project Manager Today*, October.

Luce, Edward (1997) Interview with Kenneth Clarke, *FT Weekend*, 1/2 November.

McDonald, Malcolm (1984) *Marketing Plans, How to prepare them, how to use them*, Oxford, Butterworth-Heinemann.

McDonald, Malcolm and Rogers, Beth (1998) *Key Account Management*, Oxford, Butterworth-Heinemann.

Majaro, Simon (1992) *Managing Ideas for Profit*, London, McGraw Hill Book Company Europe.

Marlow, Hugh (1994) 'Intuition and Forecasting a Holistic Approach', *Long Range Planning*, December.

Martin, Peter (date unknown) 'Stampeded into action', *Financial Times*.

Martin, Peter (1997) 'Off the beaten track', *Financial Times*, 23 January.

Mazur, Laura reviewing Ringland, Gill, (1997) *Scenario Planning: Managing for the Future*, London, John Wiley & Sons in Marketing Business.

Morita, Akio (1987) *Made in Japan*, New York, Collins.

Murdoch, Adrian (1997) 'What Fornula One taught an airline', *Management Today*, November.

Nowikowski, Frank (1997) 'Creativity = Intelligence + X', *Mensa Magazine*, April

Persaud, Raj (1997) *Staying Sane*, London, Metro Books.

Porter, Michael (1980) *Competitive Strategy*, Macmillan.

Rawsthorn, Alice (1997) 'No longer a one-man brand', *Financial Times*, 19/20 July.

Rogers, Beth (1996) *Creating Product Strategies*, London, International Thomson Business Press.

Russell, Carol and Parsons, Elizabeth, (1996) 'Putting theory to the test at the OU', *People Management*, 11 January.

Sappal, Pepi (1997) 'Emotions Running High' *BCC National Review*, March/April.

Schwartz, David (1997) 'Learning the lessons of 1987', *Financial Times*, 19 October.

Semler, Ricardo (1993) *Maverick!*, London, Century.

Senge, Peter M. (1990) *The Fifth Discipline*, New York, Doubleday.

Shaw, Robert (1997) 'Trivial Pursuits', *Marketing Business*, November.

Shutte, Lesley (1997) 'The Guru's Guru', *Director*, September.

Smith, Ian (1997) 'Avoiding future shock', *Director*, July.

Spinney, Laura (1997) 'A fate worse than death', *New Scientist*, 18 October.

Syrett and Lammiman (1997) 'The art of conjuring ideas', *Director*, April.

Sunday Mirror (1997) 'From riches to rags . . . a snip at just £2m', 23 November.

Trapp, Roger (1997) '3M: Back to the Future', *MBA*, December, Boston, Harvard Business School Press.

Utterback, James (1994) *Mastering the Dynamics of Innovation*, Boston, Harvard Business School Press.

van de Vliet, Anita, 'Gary Hamel', (magazine article, source unknown).

van der Weyer, Martin (1997) 'Corrective surgery', *Management Today*, August.

Index